GREAT IDEA
PETITE TYPEFACE
contents

Brosmind Studio — 006-015
Brosmind is a studio based in Barcelona founded by Juan and Alejandro Mingarro in 2006. Their style is fresh and optimistic and always combines fantasy and humor. Their illustrations have been awarded with the most prestigious international awards, like Cannes Lions, Clio, Eurobest, Graphis, among others... The brothers have work for clients such as Nike, Microsoft, Virgin, Gillette, Honda, Land Rover, Volkswagen, but their universe is not fully understood without their personal artistic projects, like Brosmind Army, Brosmind RV and Brosmind City.

Iqbal Hakim Boo — 016-019
Some people learn from the classroom, others from experience. For Iqbal Hakim 'Boo', those life experiences have always been his copilot at work and play. And my, what might eye candy has he produced over the years! With a knack for digital art manipulation, illustration iqbal hakim boo adds a touch of futurism and fantasy.

Jaume Osman Granda — 020-027
Jaume Osman Granda is a designer from Vilanova i la Geltrú, near Barcelona. He studied multimedia programming at the Polytechnic University in Terrassa. He first worked designing web pages and was later hired by Gominola as a flash programmer.
After a couple of years, tired of action script, he moved onto motion and started working for the Multipase studio, specialized in designing visuals for dance clubs. After some time, he started to work for the Barcelona-based studio Pornographics, where he spent two more years doing a little bit of everything, until he got tired of Barcelona and went back to his home town to work from home, where he keeps on taking part in all kinds of projects as a freelance.

Kapil Bhimekar — 028-031
Kapil Bhimekar an ex employee of Leo Burnett, Dubai is currently working with LOWE MENA as a Senior Art Director. His work has been recognized at several award shows including Cannes lions, One show, New York festivals, London International awards, Adfest Asia Pacific Dubai Lynx, etc.

Konstantin Shalev — 032-041
Creative artist, Illustrator, IOS games designer, Character designer based in Krasnodar Russia not far from black sea. After graduate with honor Kuban State University became a Freelance worker, doing jobs for some famous brands, always in search to update and develop my style of drawing. Winner of t-shirt events on Lafrarise, some of my works was printed in magazine Computer Arts Projects. Member at OFFF 11 Russian Creative Panel by Designcollector at Barcelona. Love all kinds of action sports, but skateboarding and snowboarding is my passion. Love to create colorful and bold illustration.

Marcelo Schultz — 042-049
I'm 31 years old, Graphic Designer and illustrator based in Curitiba, south of Brazil.
I work as Art Director at DDQ Design.
I build all my work from scratch and is how I like to work. I spend a lot of time drawing everything that comes into my head.
I love Technology, all about Apple Computers, and Car design!

Cuypers Sebastien — 050-053
I'm a french art director and illustrator. Born in 1980 and got used to drawing from early childhood on, in my works typography adds to the motif to make it complete but at the same time acts as an autonomous and stand-alone feature of the layout. I'm handle letters like characters, allowing for their own and strong expression. My designs are not bound to one single medium. I'm working as an art director for a communication agency as well as designing for skateboards and customizing vinyl toys. Besides that I have particular affinity to T-Shirt design which I call my 'first love'. I like the way shirts are transmitting a message or a mood according to place and situation and sees an artist designed shirt as a kind of living support for self-expression.

Ryan Bosse — 054-055
Award winning Kansas-based designer, specializing in package design, branding, illustration, typography.

Stephanie Wiehle — 056-059
Stephanie Wiehle is a freelance illustrator an graphic designer based in Berlin / Germany. After studying design (at Anhalt University of Applied Sciences in Dessau/Germany) she first started working for advertising agencies. After three years of being an art director she decided to look for new challenges. From little kid on she loves drawing and illustrating. So why don't try it as a professional artist? Since 2011 she is a freelance illustrator working for the advertising szene and different companies as well. What she does comes from the heart and she is happy with all her pencils and colours.

Matt Lyon — 060-071
Matt Lyon, aka C86, is a UK-based digital and mixed-media artist. His work explores reoccurring motifs and themes laced with wild colour combos. He has worked for the likes of Nike, AOL, AT&T, Microsoft and other global clients, and his designs have been widely seen in books, magazines and exhibitions worldwide

Tatiana Arocha — 072-075
Tatiana Arocha is a visual artist from Bogota, Colombia living in Brooklyn, New York. Her artwork combines her passion for storytelling, whether childlike or intellectual, with an incredible attention to detail and refined sense of style developed over years as a graphic designer. Arocha is also an in-demand director and illustrator for a client list ranging from ad agencies like Wieden+Kennedy and JWT to TV networks such as Sundance and Vh1 to major brands including Mitsubishi and Anthropologie.

Iglika Kodjakova — 076-077
Iglika Kodjakova is a freelance graphics designer and illustrator based in Sofia, Bulgaria. She loves to play with spots as forms, colors and associations. She inspires from seasons, her feelings and creative thoughts.

Mateusz Szulik — 078-081
Mateusz Szulik has worked in an interactive agency based in Poland for over 4,5 year as an Illustrator/animator. Now he is working as an freelance illustrator/3D artist in the game industry, making mostly concept art, illustrations, character concepts and 3D characters/environments.

Monfa — 082-083
Monfa was born Miguel Cabrera 30 years ago in Costa Rica. After drawing his way through walls and school notebooks, he decided to make a living out of illustration. He studied Fine Arts and became an editorial illustrator. His work has been featured in various websites and digital magazines, and he has also participated on different illustration projects, both national and international. Currently working on many personal projects, he splits his time between his job as an Art Director for a prestigious mexican editorial company, freelancing, art collaborations and showcasing his artwork on his personal website.

Anjo Bolarda — 084-085
Anjo Bolarda is a illustrator/designer based in Manila, Philippines. He grew up with japanese art and vintage cartoons. His works has been recognized around the world and named as one of Philippines top illustrators. He also worked with a list of clients namely Facebook, Nike, Ogilvy, Yahoo Southeast Asia, National Arts Council of Singapore, Noise Singapore, Nestle, Teesheed etc. He also exhibited works in Japan, Shanghai, Singapore, France, Belgium,Germany, New York and Spain. Anjo is also the founder of Designer of Asia. a collective of Asian illustrator and designers.And also an active contributor off GetFreaky magazine in France.

Sasha Prood — 086-093
I grew up just outside of Philadelphia, Pennsylvania, USA and trained at Carnegie Mellon's School of Design. I currently reside in a tiny studio apartment in Brooklyn, New York filled to the brim with plants. I create typography, illustrations, patterns and graphics using pencil, pen and watercolor with the computer. Thematically my works lean toward the organic, natural and scientific with vintage, utilitarian and childhood influences. Animals, vegetables and minerals of all kinds are commonly found in my illustrations, creating anything from logos to posters to apparel graphics.

Takashi Okada — 094-101
We are art direction, design and art studio based in tokyo Japan.
It was founded in 1999 by Takashi Okada.
specializing in typographical drawing and developing experimental work through motion graphics.
We work mainly in graphic design, motion graphic, illustration, interactive design field.

Teagan White — 102-111
Teagan White is a freelance designer and illustrator from Chicago, currently living and working in St Paul, Minnesota, where she recently earned her BFA in Illustration from the Minneapolis College of Art + Design. Her body of work encompasses intricate renderings of flora and fauna, playful depictions of cute anthropomorphic critters, illustrative typography, and everything in between. Her clients have included Nike, Wired Magazine, Anthropologie, Houghton Mifflin Harcourt, Target, Coca-Cola, and many small businesses, independent musicians, and individuals.

Anton Gorbunov — 112-115

I paint by hands, I like when picture looks like hand-drawn. Cos I love the inaccuracies and mistakes in any art. I think it shows the author. In spite of this I am inspired by the exact mathematical form, perfect lace in baroque style, the exact lines of graving style and typographical rhyme. I always pleased to go out on contact with interesting people, willing to participate in new projects.

Juan Osborne — 116-133

As an architect I have been involved in art and design ever since my college days. I also love programming, and new technology allows me to free my artistic side in I way which I find exciting. All of my work was done with my own tools. From my point of view creativity is also in code, because there is a human being behind that code.

AM I COLLECTIVE — 134-143

The Am I Collective is a creative studio that offers a multi-faceted, collaborative service to advertising agencies around the world.
This includes benchmark animation, illustration and typography.
Born in 2006 in the beautiful city of Cape Town, we are proudly African.
Being African feeds our natural spirit of raw adventure and this hopefully shines true in all the work we do.
Raw, and earthy in style and explorative in execution. We hope to be seen as different yet inspirational on a global platform.

André Beato — 144-151

André Beato is a Portuguese-born, London-based graphic designer and illustrator, working mostly in vector-based graphics. After receiving a B.A. in Graphic Design and an M.A. in Design Visual Culture–Visual Production from the Instituto de Artes Visuais e Marketing in Lisbon, Beato began working in his father's graphic design studio. Beginning in 2010, Beato moved to London, where he freelances for a diverse array of record labels, magazines, clothing companies, advertising and others.. Beato's use of bright colors and bold, sculptural shapes speaks to his love of mid-twentieth-century popular culture, while his finely rendered shapes reveal the influence of his father's illustrations on Beato's own practice. His 1980s-inspired graphics can be seen in Time Out London, Field & Stream magazine, and in the printed materials for Nike , Carhartt among others.

BLANQ — 152-161

With talents in all creative fields as our blocks, BLANQ is built combining creative solutions, branding, graphic design, visual styling, photography, film, ad campaigns, website design, artistic creation (illustrations and installations), and art curating, etc. Elites from various backgrounds exchange their thoughts and give birth to breakthroughs."
Acquainted with the fashion and design industry, BLANQ bands together the creative power, and realize pioneering concepts that spice up the scene. Our aesthetic vision does not retreat from commercial clichés. Our every single work has a perfect balance between creativity and expressive power, between profligacy and cultural value.

Bobby Haiqalsyah — 162-169

Bobby Haiqalsyah is a freelance graphic designer born in Indonesia but lives in Melbourne Australia. His love of comic books started his interest in the creative world, since then he has been a head chef, a martial artist, and currently works as a typographic illustrator as well as a designer. His work with type was inspired by a quote by Scott McCloud saying that "words are the highest for of abstraction". This fits with his belief and words as image has become his fascination, he credits his elaborate decorative style to the rich traditional art of the country he was born.

Brian Dixon — 170-173

Brian Dixon is one of many designers at UK based UYR group who specializes in creating concepts and artwork for clients ranging from educational bodies to the leisure industry.
Established 15 years ago in a loft, UYR has grown from humble beginnings into a successful multimedia company with over 50 employees.
UYR bases its success on reacting quickly to client demands by having it's own in-house Large Format and Litho printing facilities.

Camila Montejo — 174-181

I am a typography lover , finding it as the most dynamic and special way to work on desing. I am a passionate person in everything I do and live for my creations,doing my best in each project as if it was the first, but with the experience,patience and devotion as if it was the last.
Illustrationis a vital element that accompanies me in my day by day.
I am passionate for life, design,colors and I consider that every moment, object or circumstance has its learning, its soul and is … waiting to be heard.

Fabian de Lange — 182-189

Fabian de Lange is a 25 year old self-taught Dutch free-lance typographer, designer and art director, currently residing and working in Heerlen, The Netherlands with work experience in different creative fields of design and collaborating with clients from various industries such as clothing companies, magazines, music labels, advertising and others.

Götz Gramlich — 190-193

Götz Gramlich is 37 years old and was born and raised in heidelberg/germany. he studied communication design in darmstadt and had a longer stay at studio niklaus troxler in willisau, switzerland, which changed his views on graphic design in a very positive way! 2005 he came back to heidelberg, opened his own studio "gggrafik design". götz successfully took part in many poster competitions around the world, and got some nice prizes for his posters, like graphis gold an platinum awards, jury prize china poster biennale 2012, several 100best posters germany/austria/switzerland, red dot design award, tdc tokyo and tdc ny... actually, hes nominated for the german design award 2013.

Hugo & Marie — 194-201

Hugo & Marie is an imaginative creative agency specializing in artist management founded in early 2008. We have the pleasure of working with talented creatives who each share the compulsion to speak in the wonderful, nuanced vocabulary of visual media. We're dedicated to direction, design, illustration, interactive, and representation services to bring all manner of projects to life. This book features a selection of work by illustrators Deanne Cheuk, Jules Julien, Mario Hugo, Mike Perry, and Micah Lidberg.

Igor Mustaev — 202-207

Igor Mustaev is a type designer and lettering artist from Russia. He was born in the city of Khabarovsk in 1982. Graduated architect, he found himself more interested in working with letters, than with building plans.
In 2009 he finished the Type and Typography course at the British Higher School of Art and Design, supervised by Ilya Ruderman.
He is currently living in Moscow and working as a freelancer in graphic design, lettering and type design.

István Szugyiczky — 208-215

István Szugyiczky is a Hungarian graphic designer graduated at the Academy of Fine Arts Budapest with an MA. Working as an independent graphic designer he is interested in illustrated typography, lettering and illustration and has worked for various clients including Volkswagen, Coca Cola, Adidas, Sony Play Station, Bloomberg Markets and EMI Music.
István also made posters for charity organizations and featured in many social and environmental poster exhibitions worldwide.

Jorrit van Rijt — 216-221

Jorrit van Rijt was born September 28, 1980 in The Netherlands and now lives in Utrecht (NL). He graduated in 2006 at the Royal Academy of Art and Design in 's-Hertogenbosch.
As a graphic designer with a lot of passion for typography, he likes to experiment with shape, composition and colour to create visually strong and eccentric work. Jorrit is always in search of symbiosis between typography and image.

Max Little — 222-227

Little Fonts began in December 2012 with an intention to create unique and original display fonts. The foundry which is led by designer Max Little has a striking graphic style. Max is a young graphic designer from the UK and has a passion for strong, contemporary graphic design. His projects, both personal and those for the Little Fonts type foundry, build upon core foundations of graphic design relying on a strong use of typography as well as colour, shape, line and pattern.

Medness — 228-231

Medness loves doodling on the corners of books, ogling at guitar maestros and flipping on skateboards.
The quirky and random ideas that swarm in his head take refuge in a world known as Ahmericarnation, where they are executed in his works of illustrations, branding & identity and other graphic design projects.
If you'd like to drop by that world for some honest and collaborative fun, or any kind of creative work, drop him a message.

Mirko Camia — 232-235

Mirko Camia is an independent illustrator and digital artist based in milan italy. From 13 years old is art director of a midsize company that deals with advertising for the companies and also collaborate on two projects as a freelancer atd world studio and FRESPIRATION MAGAZINE (Chicago, USA) .The fundamental point in his illustrations and typography, which is always used with the greatest detail possible, launching increasingly strong and direct messages. at this moment is to make known my project "YOU CAN CHOOSE" the project is simply pure advertising illustration in order to raise awareness on current state of our planet.

Vladimir Tomin — 236-239

Self-taught 29 years young motion designer/illustrator from Russia, Khabarovsk. Core member of The Keystone Design Union, lead creative at MTV Russia for a year, Senior Artist at Republic Studios, Shanghai for a year. Speaker at OFFF 2011 Barcelona.

Patrick Seymour — 240-243

I like to play with vectors, construct and deconstruct things, play with symmetry, my goal is always to create simplicity and visual impact. In other words I try to make complicated visuals extremely simple.
I particularly like typography creation. I find amazing the fact that i am able to reinvent symbols that have been drawn several thousand times around the world.
26 symbols from A to Z, 26 different little logos developed within the same defined visual rules.

Philippe Nicolas   244-247

Philippe Nicolas is a french designer specializing in a wide range of disciplines - illustration, graphic design, branding, art direction, and typography. Multilingual and multifaceted, his creative imagery and precise design has led to close relationships with renowned clients around the globe.
The last years, Philippe has worked internationally, from San Francisco to Milan. With a wide range of experience in different creative fields, the power of his work is based in a deep knowledge of client and agency business and a quick, straightforward approach to results. He currently works and resides in Turin, Italy.

Photonica   248-253

Maria Isabel Macías Llorente
When I finished the university I realized that I really want to be a graphic designer, I hate my career, and I found in graphic design the best way to express myself, especially by typography art. I love painting new shapes of typography and creating posters with lyrics. I hope still doing this all my life.
Everything I know I learnt it by myself, I think it's the best way to learn.

Toby and Pete   254-259

Toby and Pete is a team of talented creatives, designers and crafts people working together across a range of mediums.
Sharing a belief that a good creative mind can tackle any problem across any discipline we draw input from all our team on all projects. Our key focus is innovative visual direction and we push ourselves to develop new approaches to image creation.
Our love for creative collaboration means we not only share our skills sets internally, we also call upon the talents of creatives that extend beyond the core of Toby and Pete. This means that we are able to produce a diverse folio whilst keeping a consistent direction and approach to our work.

Ágnes Jekli and Anikó Kőhegyes   260-265

Ágnes Jekli and Anikó Kőhegyes are Budapest based graphic designerers, currently doing their MA studies together at MOME (Moholy-Nagy University of Art and Design). The AGIKO project gave a possibility for their teamwork, and finding the synthesis in their ars poetica.

Bao Nguyen   266-269

Since my introduction to graphic design during my sophomore year of high school I have desired to make it my career. In addition to my education background and training, I also spend many hours experimenting on my own with different graphic applications. I am constantly pushing myself to learn the elements of design such as color, emphasis, layout, and--especially--typography. The first client I worked with was in 2006, and I have steadily gained more over time. The feeling gained from creatinganything, from a simple logo to a large promotional poster, is extremely satisfying. Knowing that whenever someone sees and enjoys my work is an extremely gratifying experience.

Niels Buschke   270-281

SANTIAGO DESIGN
Design studio SANTIAGO DESIGN was founded in 2002 by Niels Buschke. From small, privately owned companies to large multinational corporations, SANTIAGO DESIGN delivers innovative and unique design solutions to achieve impact in competitive markets. As logos are drawn, colour palettes are defined and fonts are crafted, a distinctive brand world is created to communicate the values of the client.
SANTIAGO DESIGN continues to engage in a broad range of design, branding and corporate appearances, offering clients a unique blend of obsessive attention to detail and high artistic standards with a detail-oriented execution.

Anthony Gargasz   282-289

I am a 20 year old artist & designer fascinated with digital creation. It all began when I stumbled upon Photoshop on a friends computer, and from that day forward I became obsessed with what you could create using your mind and a machine. My skill set is mainly self taught with about a month of college education that really filled in a lot of blanks on basics that I had never learned. I'm very passionate towards digital art & it's progression. I am currently an administrator of the international media collective EvokeOne, and contributor to the popular design blog Other Focus. As for my personality you could say I'm very outgoing, enthusiastic, and optimistic. I believe that life is too short to be serious all of the time, so I try to focus on making others laugh, smile, and enjoy life.

Anthony Neil Dart   290-293

Anthony Neil Dart is an independent image-maker living and working in Johannesburg South Africa, Anthony explores mostly graphic design, typography, illustration, photography, motion design and digital design. Anthony has well over a decade of experience working with clients around the world and has been featured in many publications and websites around the globe.

Filter017   294-301

Filter017 created since 2004.
Our team consists of Mixed Sauce & Wonder Work + 99% passion towards creation.
We infuse unique graphics into all kinds of design.

Josip Kelava   302-309

My art teacher once said, "The worst thing a designer can do is not get noticed." From those words, I realized that it wasn't so much about making something look good, but creating an emotional response that meant more than just a pretty picture. With this motivation, I continued to push myself to make my work bold, confident and memorable.
As a Croatian born designer, I have lived most of my life in Australia's design capital, Melbourne. My direction towards the design world connects with my passion for photography, my lust for typography and the thrill of creating something from nothing.

Keetra Dean Dixon   310-313

Artist & designer Keetra Dean Dixon straddles a wide set of mediums in her irreverent and sometimes process-intensive work. Her projects are spurred on by the fallibility of communication, attempts to connect, and shortcomings of creative tools. Dixons work has been featured in GOOD Magazine, exhibited as part of the 2009 U.S. Presidential Inauguration, and is currently showing at the Walker Art Center & the Smithsonian's Cooper-Hewitt, National Design Museum.

Kissmiklos   314-317

Designer and visual artist
Currently the architecture, design and graphic design are his workfields. There is an outstanding aesthetic quality and strong artistic approach characterizing his implementation of work. His fine artworks define his work just as the individual perceptioned corporate identity designs and graphics (listed) under his name.

Travis W. Simon   318-321

Travis Simon is a designer, sign painter and typographer living in Brooklyn, NY. Since receiving his BFA from the School of Visual Arts in 2006, Travis has remained active in graphic design, illustration, and type design. Simon's focus on hand lettering and illustrative exploration affords him numerous opportunities to create outside of the digital world. His work is derived from traditional sign painting, 1960s New York advertising and an overall respect for the old school methods. Currently he's looking forward to building up his new sign painting business and keeping up his steady process of making something new every day.

Yanina Arabena and Guillermo Vizzari   322-327

Yani Arabena and Guille Vizzari were born in Buenos Aires, Argentina. Graphic Designers, they first met in a world surrounded by inks and notebooks. Colours and textures. Nibs and pens. Letters and illustrations that today indeed fill their lives.

Craig Ward   328-335

Craig Ward is a British-born, New York based designer who likes playing with words. Having worked at a handful of design and advertising agencies in london, he eventually moved to New York to found his collaborative studio, Words are Pictures. In love with language, he has relentlessly pursued the notion of word as image for a variety of clients from the publishing, fashion and music industries. A regular contributor to several industry journals, his work has been shown and documented globally in countless magazines, books and exhibitions.

Less GRRR more WEEE Brosmind Studio Client: Virgin Active

Illustration for Virgin Active gyms promotional campaign.

Hello healthy babies

Illustration for a (RED) charity campagin.

Brosmind Studio

Illustrator: Brosmind

Jelly — Brosmind Studio — Client: Dave Matthews Band

Limited edition poster for Dave Matthews Band concert in Irvine, CA.

For all the headaches along the way   Brosmind Studio   Illustrator: Brosmind

Branded artwork for a regular under 18's clubbing event held at various nightclubs in the UK.

MMJ *poster* — Brosmind Studio — Client: My Morning Jacket

Limited edition poster for My Morning Jacket.

Slightly Stoopid — Brosmind Studio — Client: Slightly Stoopid

Limited edition poster for Slightly Stoopid.

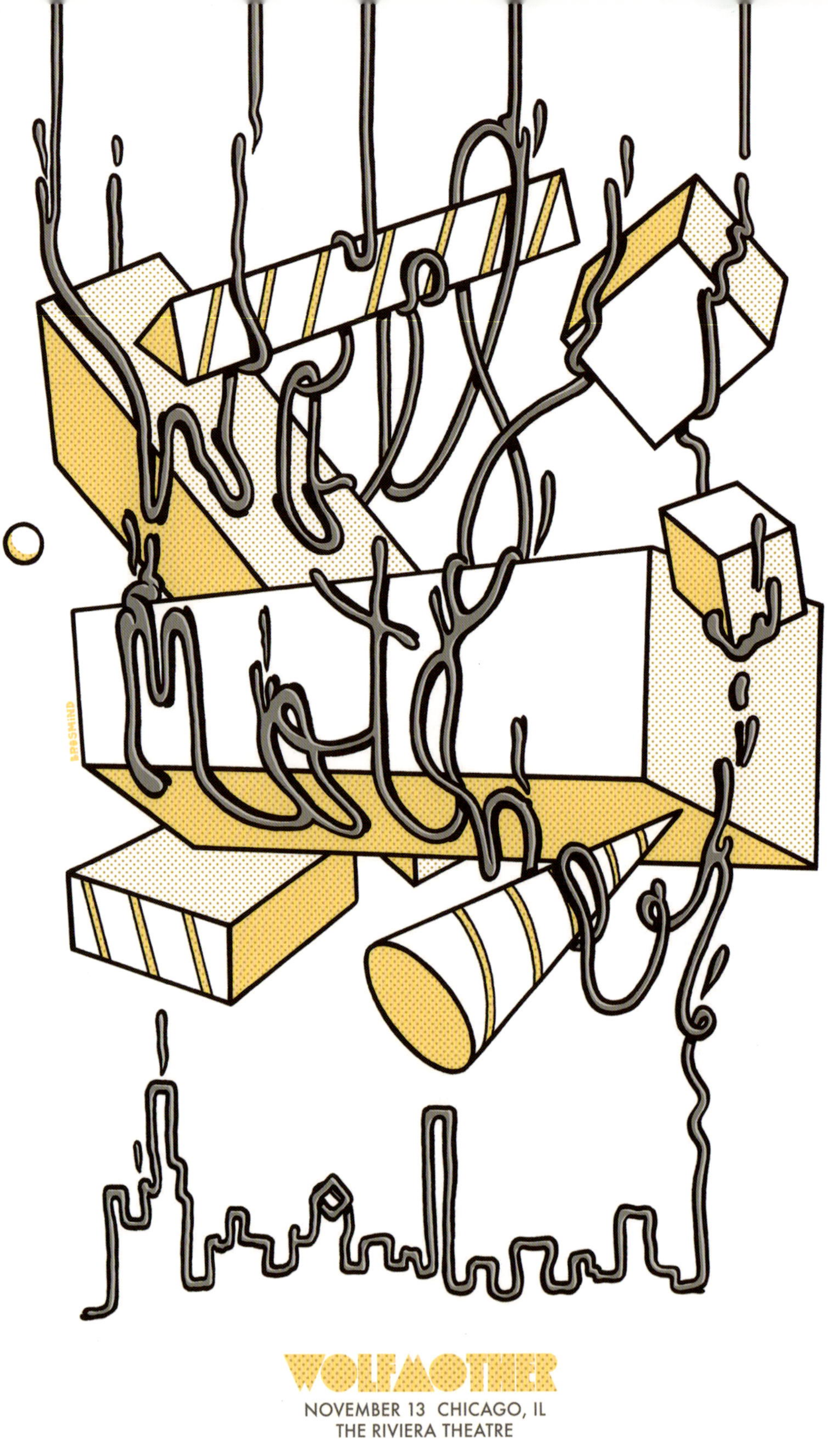

Wolfmother gigposters — Brosmind Studio — Client: Wolfmother

Limited edition posters for Wolfmother concerts in NY, Chicago and London.

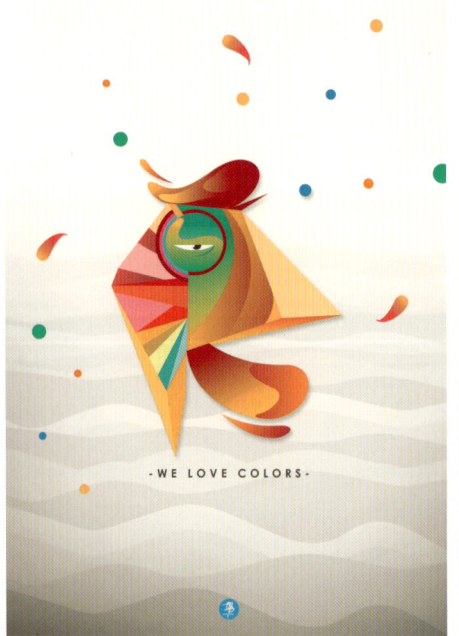

WE LOVE COLORS

Iqbal Hakim Boo

Tool: Photoshop and Illustrator
Geometric pattern and variation of colour is used for this artwork. its for the "We Love Color" poster contest a couple month ago.
Im mix up the typo with the animal element that suit for the shape such as bird, bear, prawn, owl, chicken head, deer, whale and so on referring to the image.

The Letter "S" Iqbal Hakim Boo

Tool: Photoshop and 3ds max
It start when im playing around with 3dsmax software, i put a few basic shape like square, rectangle, circle and applying some effect. It turns to abstract look alike, messy, then, i was thinking to make a typography from the shape that i made.
So, i choose letter 'S' because it was the nearest shape that look alike.
After that, i render, took it and place it in photoshop to finalise, put some lighting effect, color blend and shadowing.

CROMOK

Iqbal Hakim Boo

Tool: Adobe Illustrator and Photoshop.
Cromok is a trash metal band here in Malaysia, This artwork is just a tribute to them,. I took a reference from their old album cover, it's a unicorn.
Then, I made a new one in my way, my own imagination, stars making the shape in vector, then finished it in photoshop, blend it with variety of colors
and mix it with polygonal/geometrical shape,
And multiply the grunge texture on top. Done.somehow it doesn't looks like a thrash metal taste.

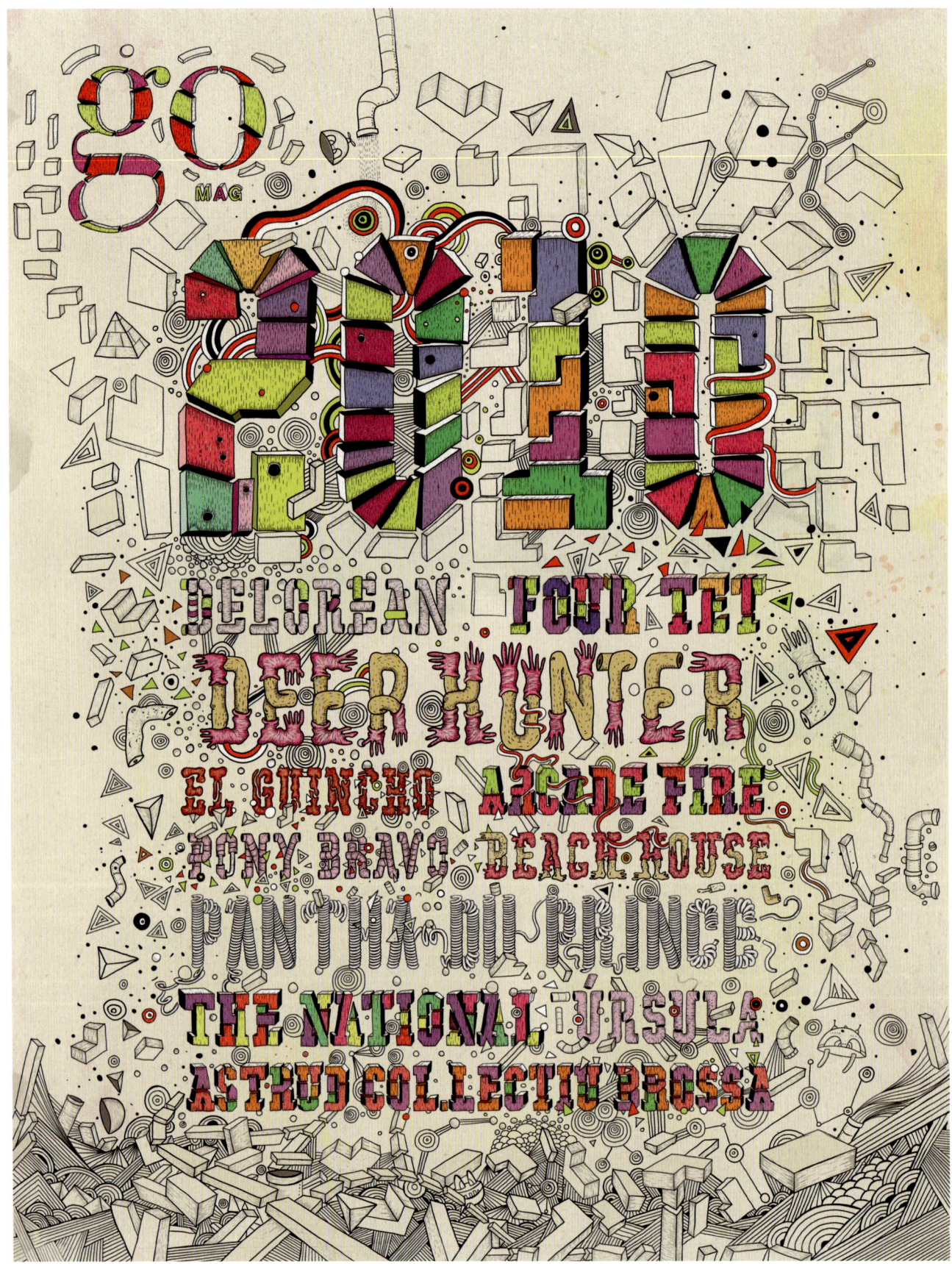

Go Magazine

Jaume Osman Granda

Client: Go Magazine

Cover design for Go Mag magazine.

CUBITUS REGULAR　　　　　　　　Jaume Osman Granda

Personal illustration

DrogaEstereo

Jaume Osman Granda

Client: DrogaEstereo

Art direction and design for the hip hop band Drogaestereo.

BC BRUTA Jaume Osman Granda Client: bc bruta

Illustratation for a collective

Suite Momo Jaume Osman Granda Client: Suite Momo

Art direction and design for the punk band Suite Momo.

Suite Momo

Poster design for the band SuiteMomo.

Jaume Osman Granda

Client: Suite MOmo

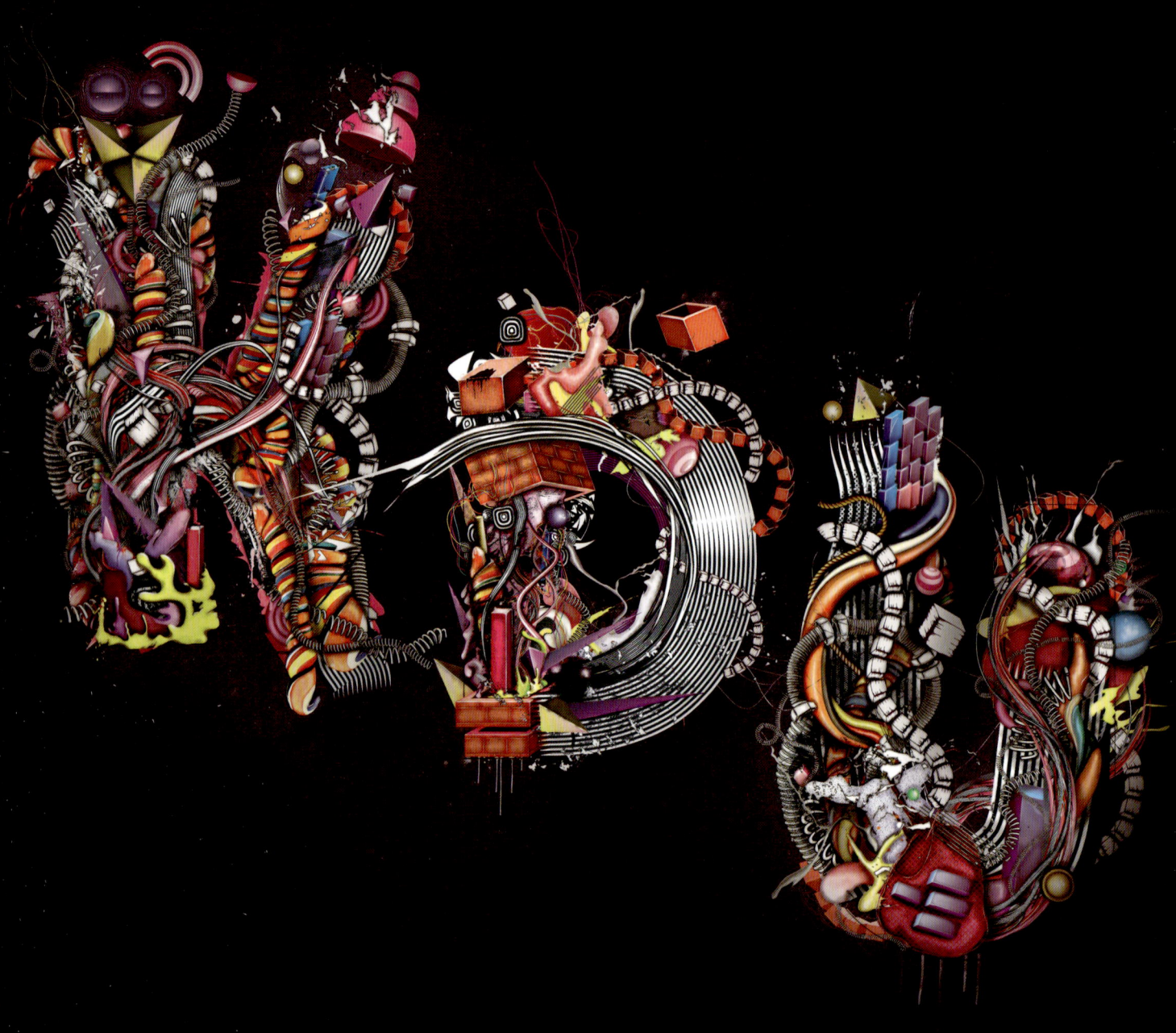

KDU

Jaume Oman Granda

Client: KDU

Illustration for The KDU.

Vicelona — Jaume Osman Granda — Client: Vicelona

T Shirt design for Vicelona.

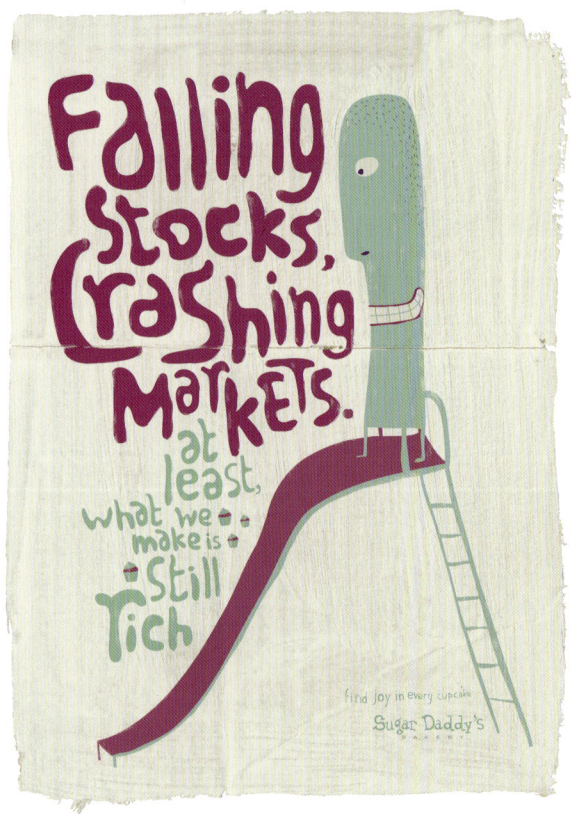

Sugar Daddy's Bakery posters

A series of in store posters designed for Sugar Daddy's Bakery in Amman, Jordan

Kapil Bhimekar

Design Agency: Leo Burnett, Dubai
Creative Director: Yayati Godbole
Client: Sugar Daddy's bakery
Copy writer: Clevin Antao

Sugar Daddy's Bakery Packaging

Kapil Bhimekar

Design Agency: Leo Burnett, Dubai
Creative Director: Yayati Godbole
Client: Sugar Daddy's bakery
Copy writer: Jaison Ben

Brief: Sugar Daddy's bakery is famous for its unique cupcakes. Chefsare constantly inventing new recipes and adding it to the menu every month. The bakery wanted this uniqueness to reflect in their packaging too.

Idea: We quantified what the taste buds of our customers experienced. Sofor example if a cake that offered a surprise in every bite weighed 1200grams, the packaging would read, '1200 grams of surprise'. We created 11different packaging designs that were fresh, engaging and playful byusing interesting typography and illustration.

Results: Customers always had a sweet smile when they saw the one-worddescription illustrated on the packaging. They even started collectingthese cake boxes and were constantly on the lookout for new cake box designs.

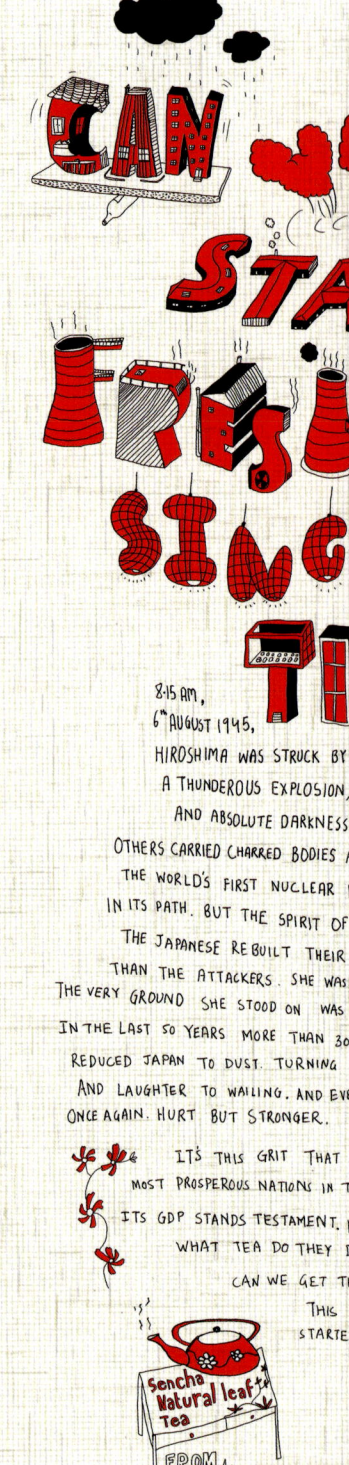

Awan Tea Posters

Kapil Bhimekar

Keeping in mind the Arab spring and the 'wave of change' that the Lebanese people demand, we created a campaign that brings inspiring stories from each country. These are real life stories that have brought about change in their respective nations. The design borrows from the culture and history of each country. The typography captures the essence of the story. Indication of how successful the outcome was in the market: The customers were in awe of the posters. They demanded that a poster be given along with each purchase of tea. Humbled by the public demand Awan tea gave out posters with a purchase of 1kg tea. Customers even began taking pictures of the posters and uploading it on facebook, this created lot of curiosity and increased footfall in the Awan store in Lebanon.

Design Agency: Leo Burnett, Dubai
Creative Director: Yayati Godbole
Client: Awan Tea, Lebanon
Copy writer: Jaison Ben

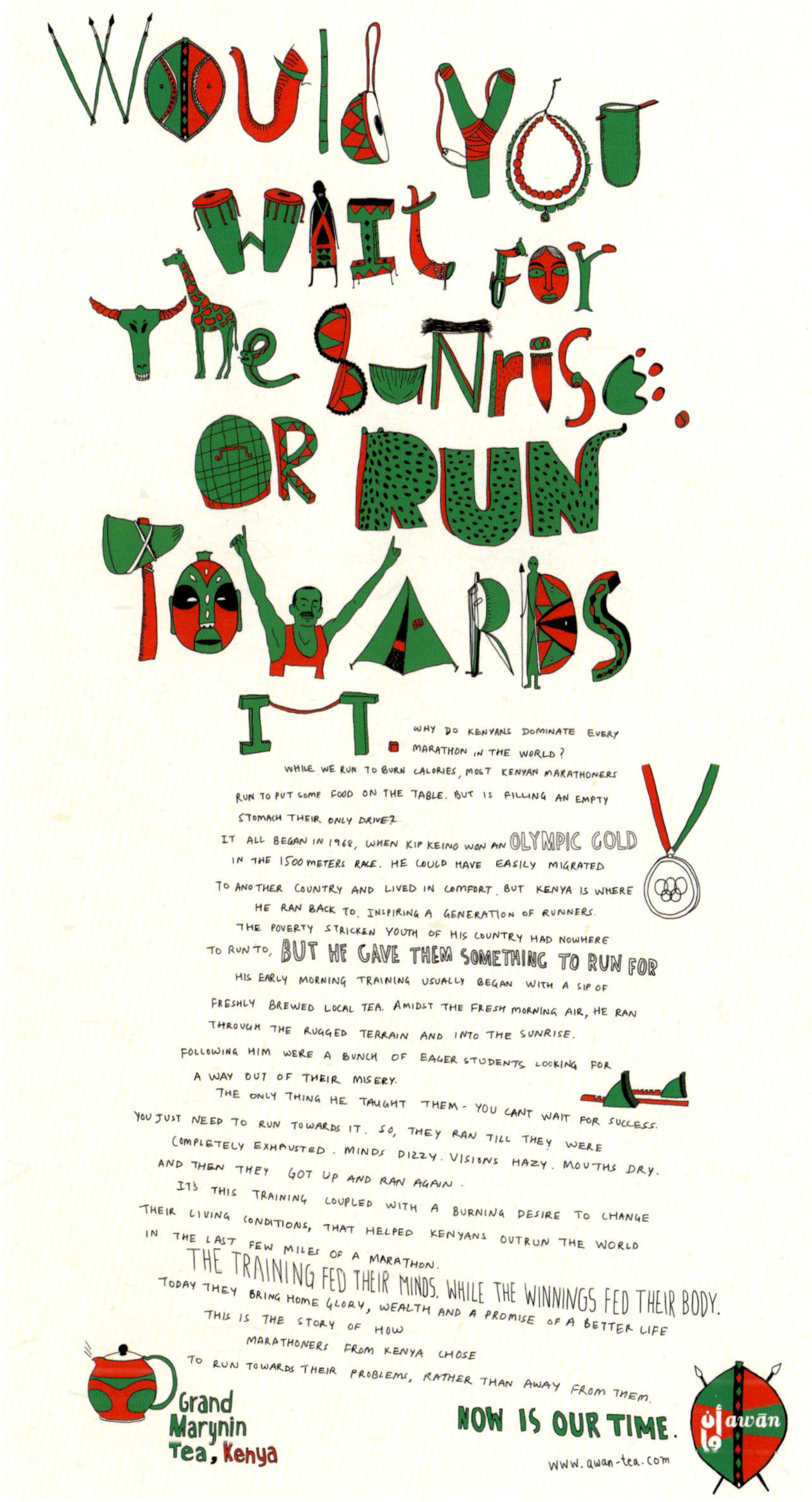

CAR VINYL PATTERN

Customer pattern work.

KONSTANTIN SHALEV aka KVADART

tops

SNOWBOARDS series *"VICE"*   KONSTANTIN SHALEV aka KVADART

Customer job, snowboards design for ENDEAVOR SNOWBOARDS

FRESH CHARACTERS

KONSTANTIN SHALEV aka KVADART

Personal project, characters set and fresh typography, pattern work.

FRESH CHARACTERS   KONSTANTIN SHALEV aka KVADART

Personal project, characters set and fresh typography, pattern work.

Born To Shine Marcelo Schultz

This work was inspired by the colors.

Coffee Lovers Marcelo Schultz

Poster using the theme "Coffee". Are you a Coffee fan? So am I. I always have a cup of coffee between me and my work.

DDQ Design　　　　　　　　　　　Marcelo Schultz　　　　　　　　　　　Client: DDQ Design

Lettering to wall of Design Office "DDQ Design"

Do It Yourself — Marcelo Schultz

Wooden Poster Style

Hold On Marcelo Schultz

The idea here is desconstruct the type

Nike – Just Do It

Marcelo Schultz

Experimental design for T-shirts. Not for sale purposes.

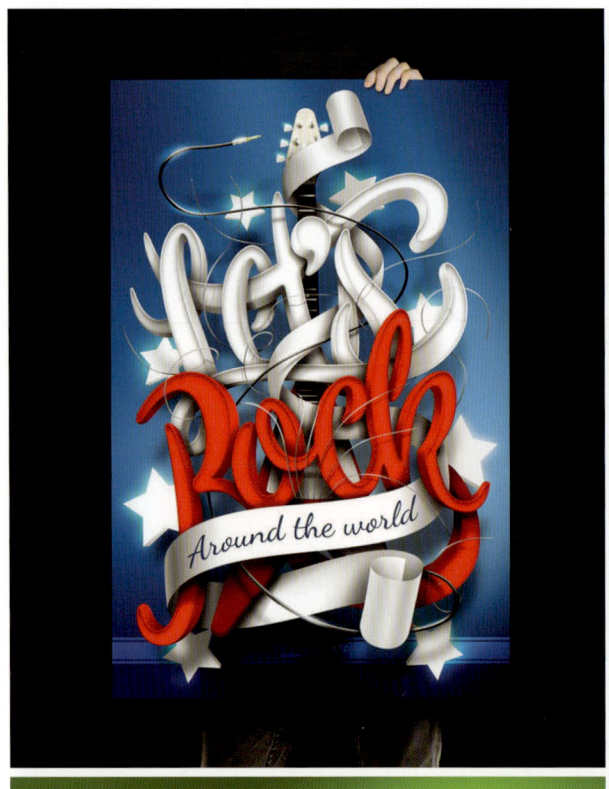

Let's Rock Around The World   Marcelo Schultz

Illustrated Poster about Rock!

Lost Empire   Marcelo Schultz

Poster created using antique ornaments and textures.

Save The Nature   Marcelo Schultz

It's very urgent to start our protest against pollutions and other harms, which attack our earth. Save our nature and thereby save our earth.

Nike – Just Do It Marcelo Schultz

Experimental project, not for sale purposes. The idea of this illustration is bring the colors and style of the 90's sneakers.

Shadowness Marcelo Schultz

Gothic Style poster

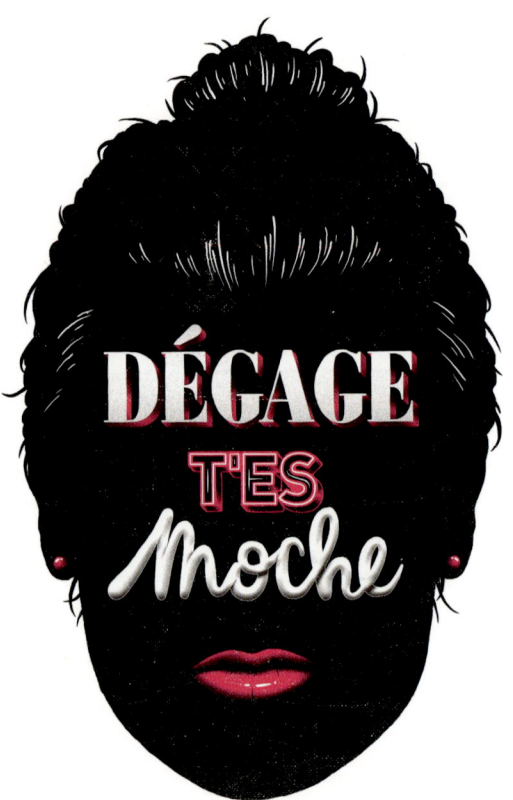

Bien le bonjour Cuypers Sebastien

Creation of 3 designs for a t-shirt contest.

Cocacola Cuypers Sebastien

Creation for an Asian Cocacola contest.

Montana

Cuypers Sebastien

Personal project around the MTN 94 Spray Paint.

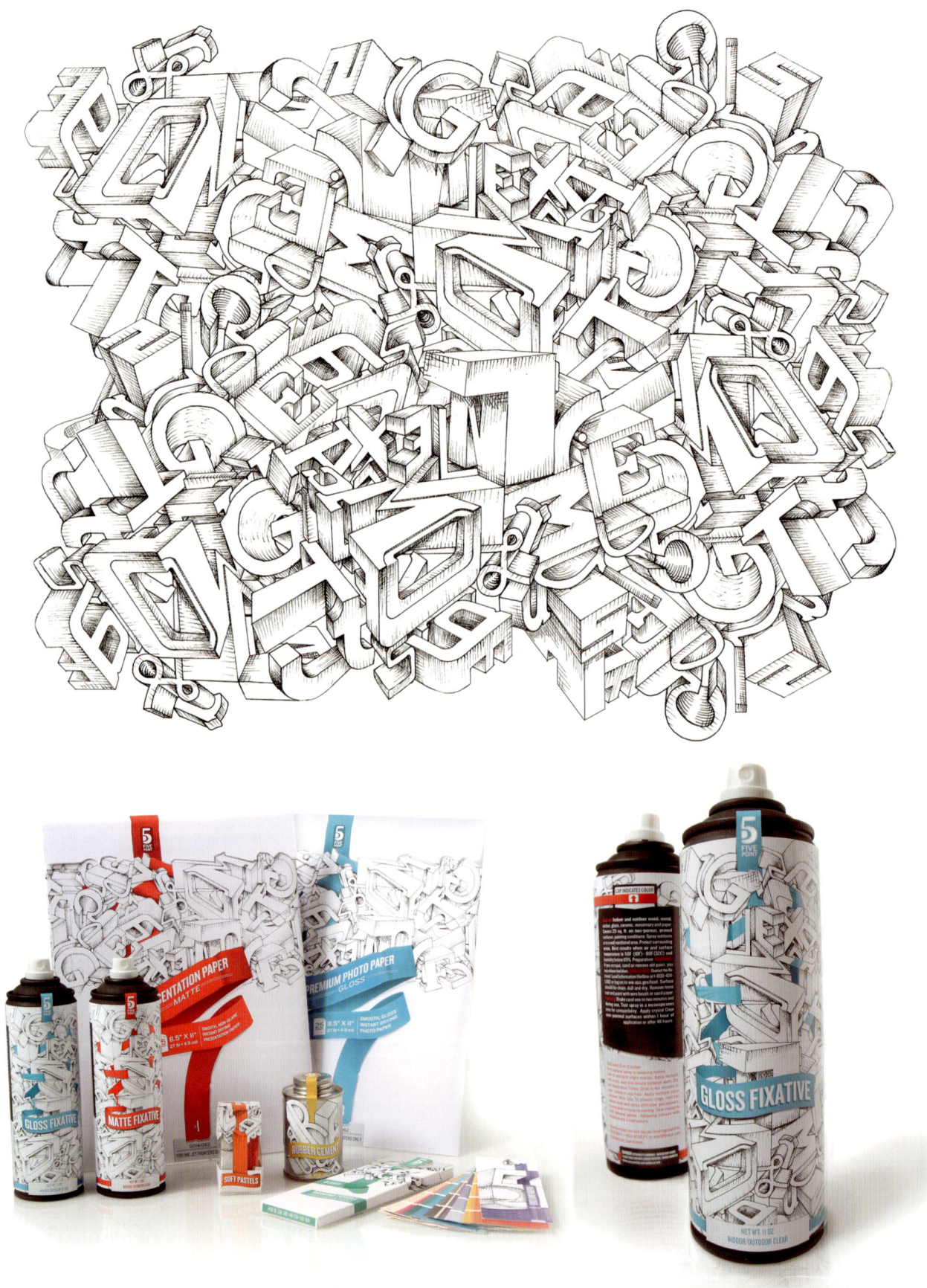

Five Point Art supplies

Ryan Bosse

Five Point art supplies are art products that appeal to the 20 to 40 year old artist. The in-store idea is that the detailed design will immediately catch the eye of any artist, being that every artist is detail oriented in someway. The design is unique enough that no matter what isle in the store, when you see the elaborate design you automatically relate it to the great product you bought from Five Point previously.

Inspiration Calendar

Ryan Bosse

This calendar is for anyone who wants to get more out of each day of their lives. Using the framework of toy model pieces, you pop out a piece each day and build a different flying machine for each month, thus giving flight to all your inspirations. Each month has left over pieces of inspiration for each individual to do with what they like. Each pack contains 6 different months, that build 6 different flying machines.

The christmas SIGG bottle   Stephanie Wiehle   Client: Jung von Matt/Neckar, Germany

The brief was to do an illustration for a SIGG™ bottle, the attendant package plus a little greeting card. The idea was to send it out to more than 200 clients of Jung von Matt / Neckar advertising agency as a christmas gift for 2010.
For me it was important to represent Jung von Matt as the sender of the gift in an unusual way. The drawn horse on the bottle is an illustrated version of JvM's agency logo, the Trojan horse. I liked the idea to change it in a freaky and funny way since the whole gift should appear so joyful and colourful. It shouldn't look like an ordinary give-away! I started some sketches with pencils on paper. After choosing the one I built it anew with Illustrator because the drawing on the bottle needed to be a vector image for the silkscreen print production. The art and typography of the package and card is hand drawn, too and colored in Photoshop.

The christmas tree bauble

Stephanie Wiehle

Client: Jung von Matt/Neckar, Germany

I was asked by the advertising agency Jung von Matt / Neckar again to illustrate another christmas give away: A christmas tree bauble plus the package and a little greeting card. It should be for the agency clients and the staff of Jung von Matt / Neckar.
After people liked the christmas SIGG bottle illustration style so much i should use the same style for the bauble again. That extraordinary christmas tree decoration needed to be colourful, joyful and funny. Andof course the agency logo – the Trojan horse – plays a role again so that everybody knows who the sender is!
It was a blast to start doing the sketches while having that in mind. For me as a type lover it was important to use nice ornamental letterings which matches to the comic styled illustrations. The bauble perfectly fits in its package. I hope it brings a smile to the face of every recipient.

Type and Nature Stephanie Wiehle

I really like type illustrations with a lot of ornaments and details. This work shows written words totally integrated into natural elements like plants, leafs and branches. Just the colours make the difference between them.

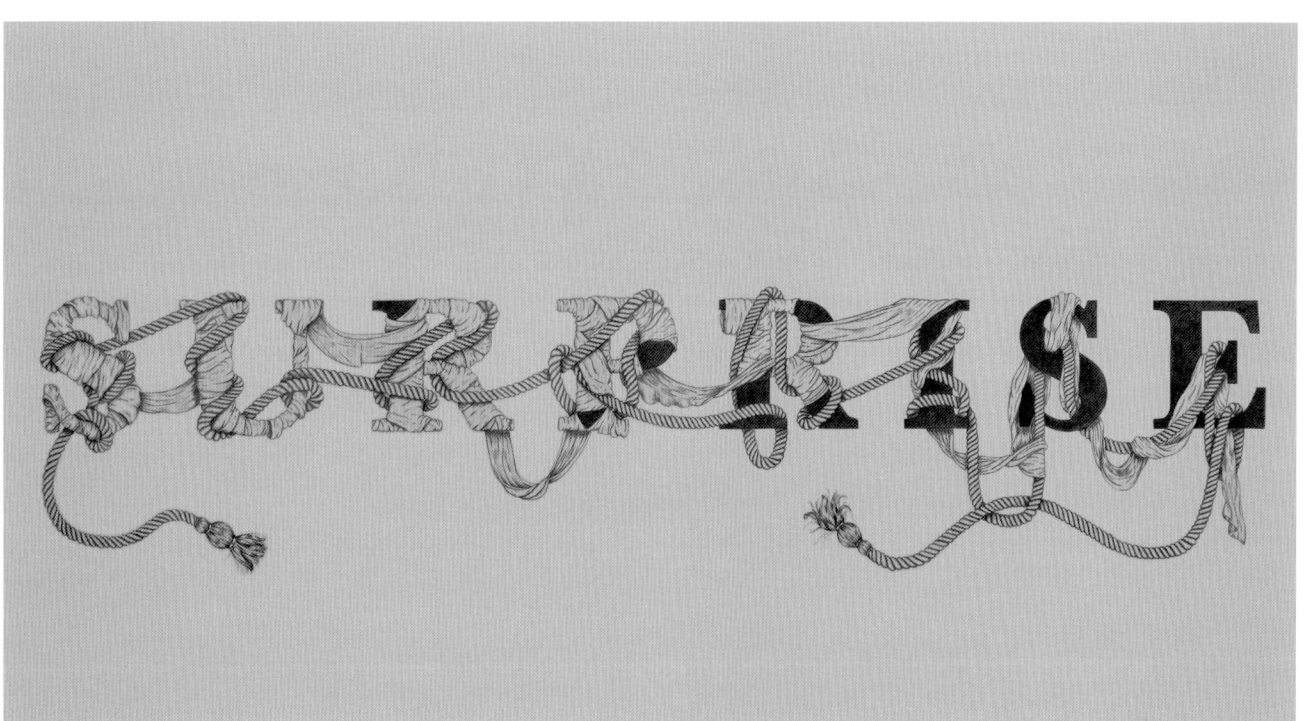

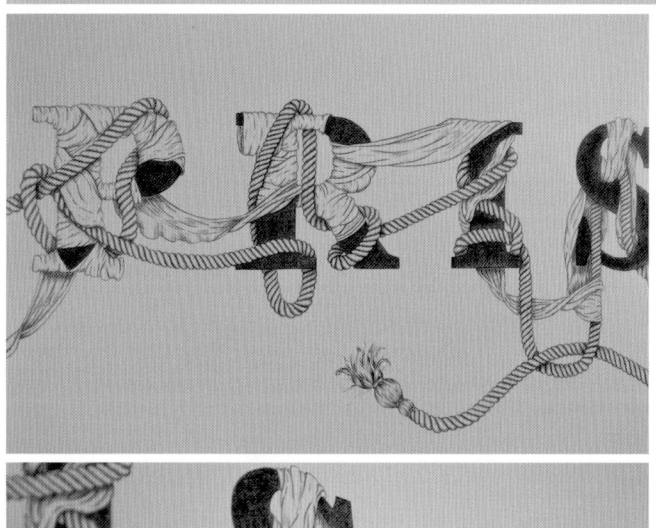

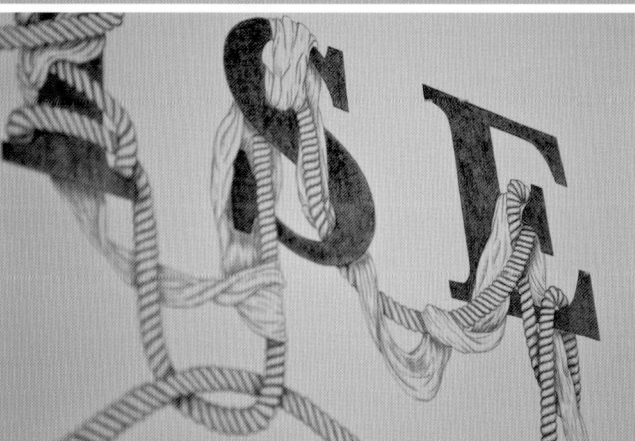
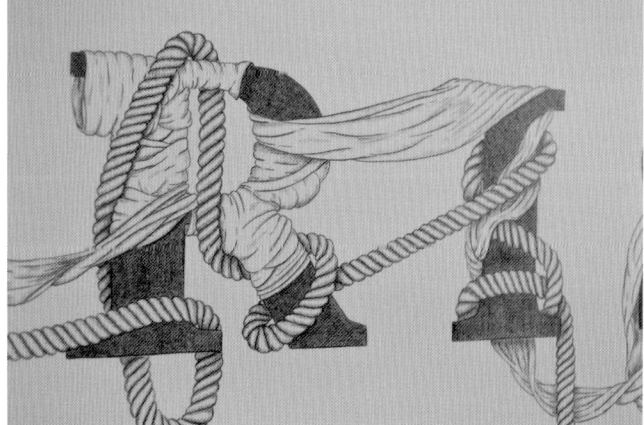

Type illustration «SURPRISE»　　　　　　　　　　　　　　　Stephanie Wiehle

I love typography and use every chance to do personal work. This time i wanted to draw something ultra real just with graphite. The work includes a little message and shows the meaning of the written word. The original size of the format is about 34 inches long. It took me a whole while to finish the drawing but it was kind of relaxing to me.

Daily Drawings Matt Lyon

Taken from a personal daily project of 365 designs for 2011, comprising of typography, illustration and abstract works

Daily Drawings Matt Lyon

Taken from a personal daily project of 365 designs for 2011, comprising of typography, illustration and abstract works

Personal Works Matt Lyon

Ongoing experiments exploring illustrative typography and font design

Pack my box with five dozen liquor jugs.
0 1 2 3 4 5 6 7 8 9 =

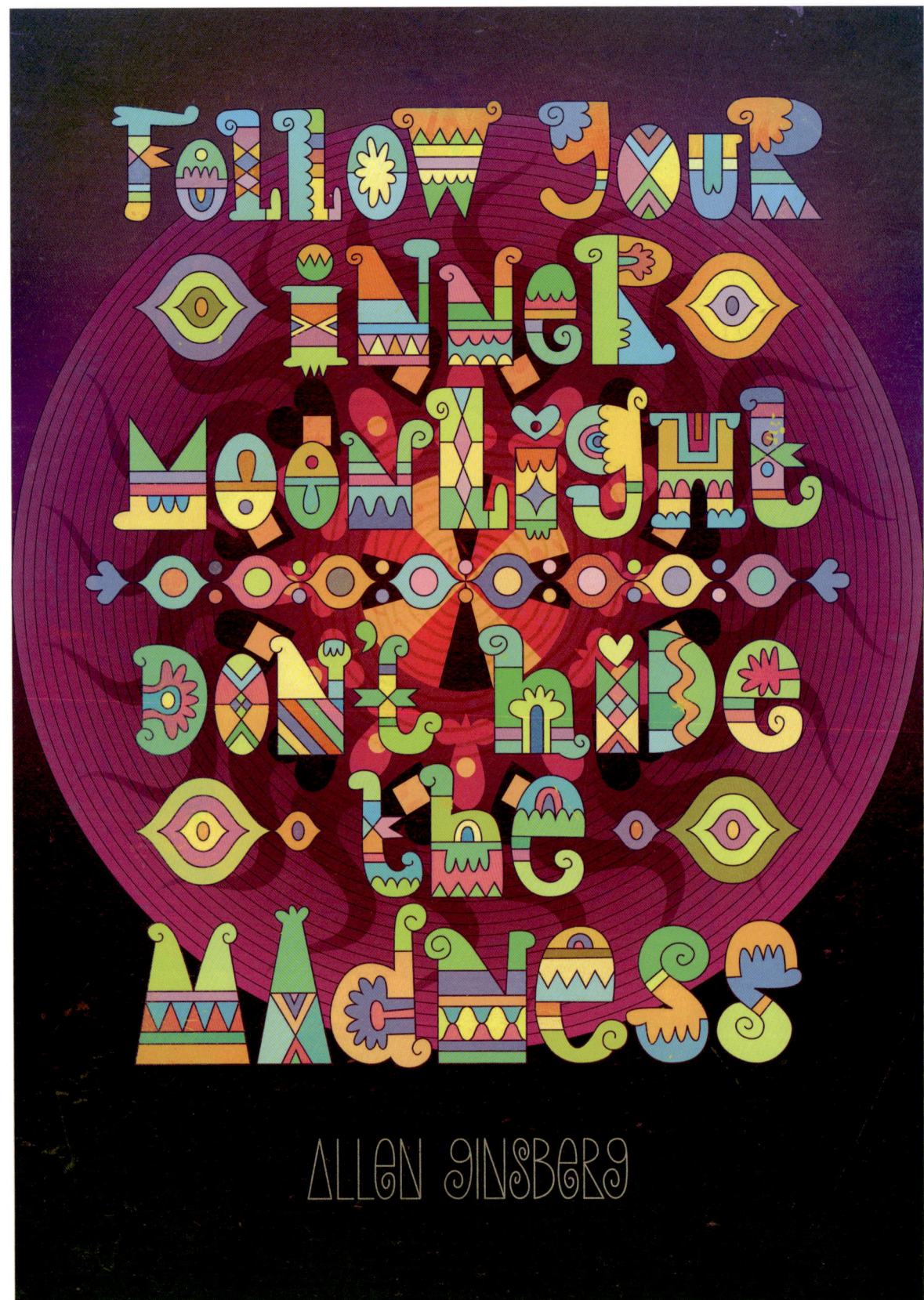

Typoquotes — Matt Lyon

Taken from an ongoing series of designs, dubbed 'typoquotes', that display quotations or sayings with illustrative type

KINDNESS IN GIVING CREATES LOVE

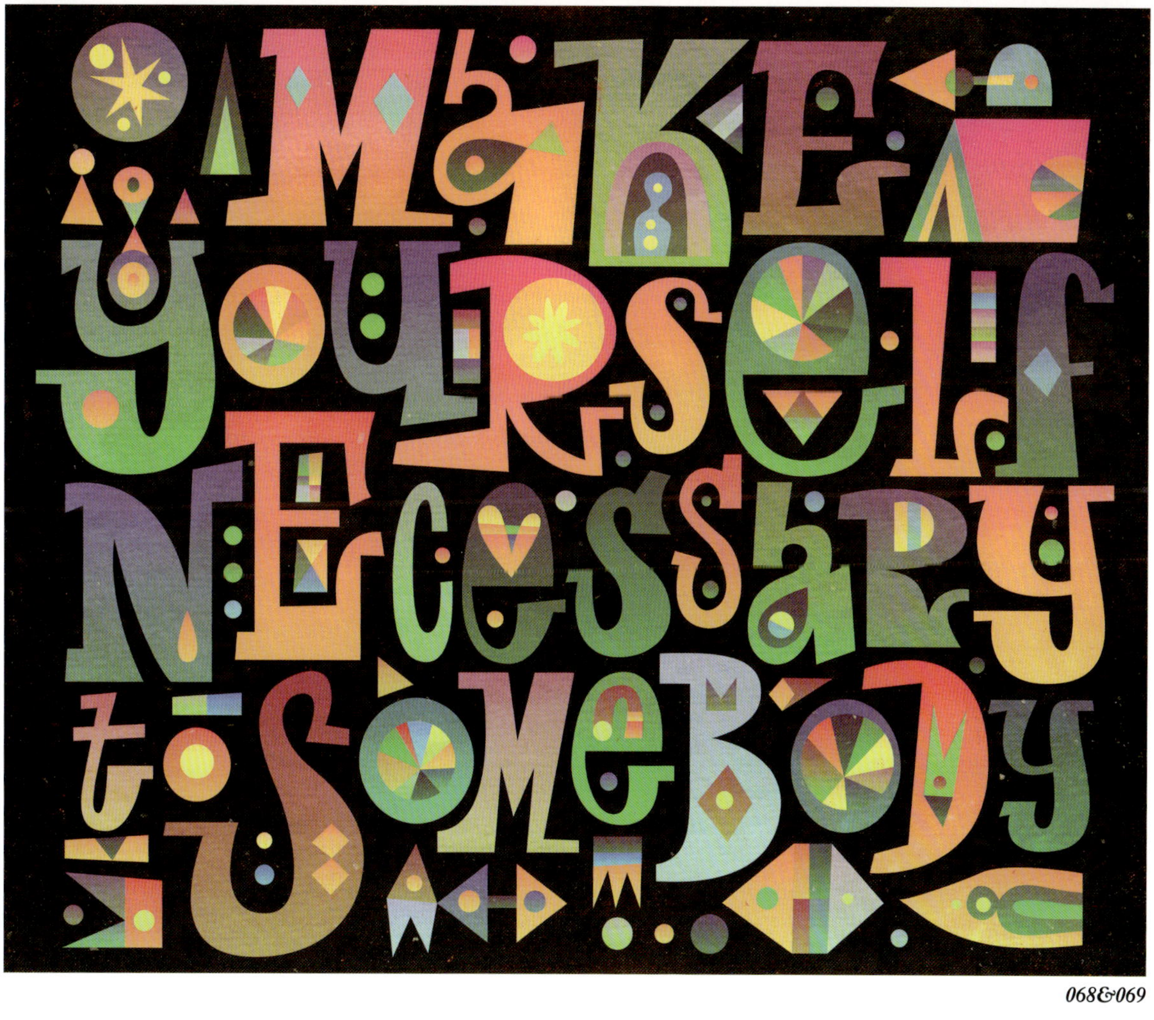

MAKE YOURSELF NECESSARY TO SOMEBODY

Paragon Matt Lyon Client: Wheatpaste Art Collective

Custom alphabet for a range of letter-based wall decals

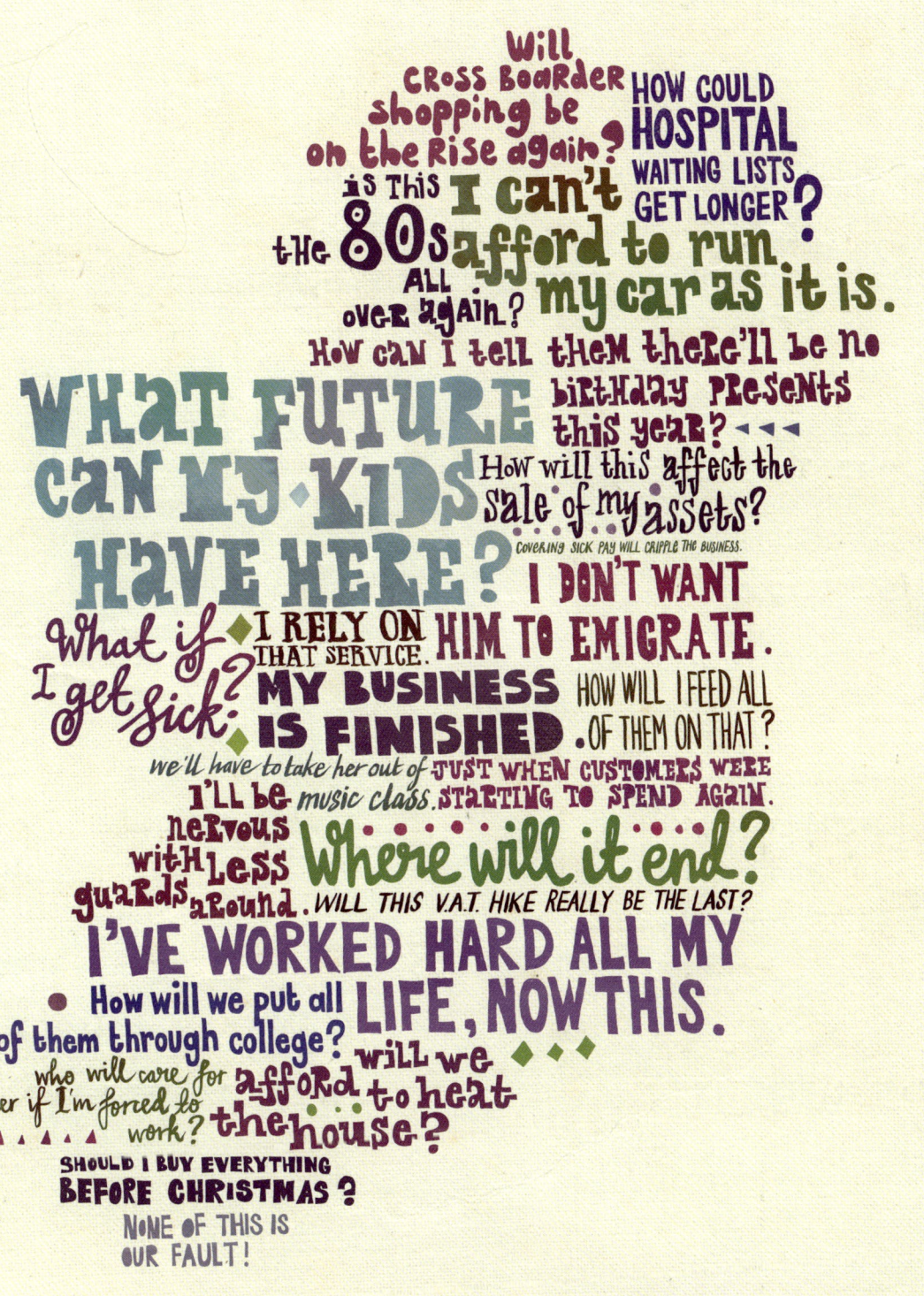

Where Will it End? — Matt Lyon — Client: Irish Examiner

Full page editorial illustration for the Irish Examiner, a broadsheet newspaper

Acopladitos Logo and Promotional Poster Tatiana Arocha Client: Acopladitos

Identity for Acopladitos a Spanish immersion music program for young children based in New York City.

Acopladitos Book Cover and Internal Pages — Tatiana Arocha — Client: Acopladitos

Artwork for Acopladitos songbook.

ABCdario, Contemos Hasta 10, Tasting Menu, Amigos   Tatiana Arocha

Educational Kids' Posters

Animal Typography, Numbers in action Iglika Kodjakova

Animal Typography: In this animal alphabet the small ones will discover that each vivid letter sign corresponds to the first letter of the animal name in English therein and they will learn and enjoy the experience.
Numbers in action: A funny educational numerical set. The kids should count the elements in each numerical sign and eventually discover that the signs match precisely what they've counted.

TypoNimals   Mateusz Szulik

This project was created because of two simple motives: I was totally bored with all educational resources used at school to teach children letters and numbers, and I love to make illustrations for kids. So we (my wife helped me a lot with ideas) decided to make a polish alphabet, where each character is visualized as an animal. We tried to figure out such an animals, where showed letter would be the first letter of the animal name, and this idea succeeded in almost all cases (I know I know, you could say that Yeti is not an animal ;)). Of course animals names are in polish language.
Software used: 3ds max, Vray, Photoshop

TypoNimals   Mateusz Szulik

Mascaradas — Monfa

Typography «mascaradas»
Characters from traditional parade.
There are some giants with wooden legs and masks dancing, running down the village street: good demons, ladies, characters from legends, to any product of the imagination with legs, a little place called Costa Rica.

MONFA

A B C D E F G H I J K L M N O P Q R S T U V W X Y Z

Numbers / Con Artist — Anjo Bolarda — Client: Con Artist

Black X White series is another illustration style i created. Along with Dum Gun Juju, Nasties and Imaginary Doodles. Black X White is focus more on eclectic black and white patterns and cross culture inspired illustrations.
Numbers is a collection i created for Con Artist, a collective workspace and retail store located at 119 Ludlow street, Basement.

Mushroom URL — Sasha Prood — Illustrator/Letterer – Sasha Prood

This hand lettering was created in 2010 for self-promotion.

MANIMALS — Sasha Prood — Client: Maxim Magazine

This typographic illustration was created in 2011 for Maxim Magazine's April issue. It was used as the title of a humor feature introducing its audience to 'the actual x-men'.

Flora Lettering — Sasha Prood — Illustrator/Letterer – Sasha Prood

These typographic illustrations were created in 2010 as personal explorations.

Hello Sasha Prood Illustrator/Letterer – Sasha Prood

This lettering was created in fall 2011 and printed on postcards for use as a self-promotional mailer.

Catch Me If U Can Sasha Prood Illustrator/Letterer – Sasha Prood

This painting was created in 2011 as part of an ongoing personal project to design a set of scarves to be sold on my online web shop, the Print Shop.

Botanica Caps — Sasha Prood — Illustrator/Letterer – Sasha Prood

This hand lettering was created in 2010 for self-promotion. It has since attracted the attention of several retailers including HandMadeFont and Arty People!, who have sold it as both a non-keyable font and a poster.

Dream Big — Sasha Prood — Client: the Say Something Poster Project

This poster was created in 2010 at the request of the Say Something Poster Project (project founder, Jason Stevens) for their first annual charity poster contest. Designers were asked to create a poster that would inspire children.

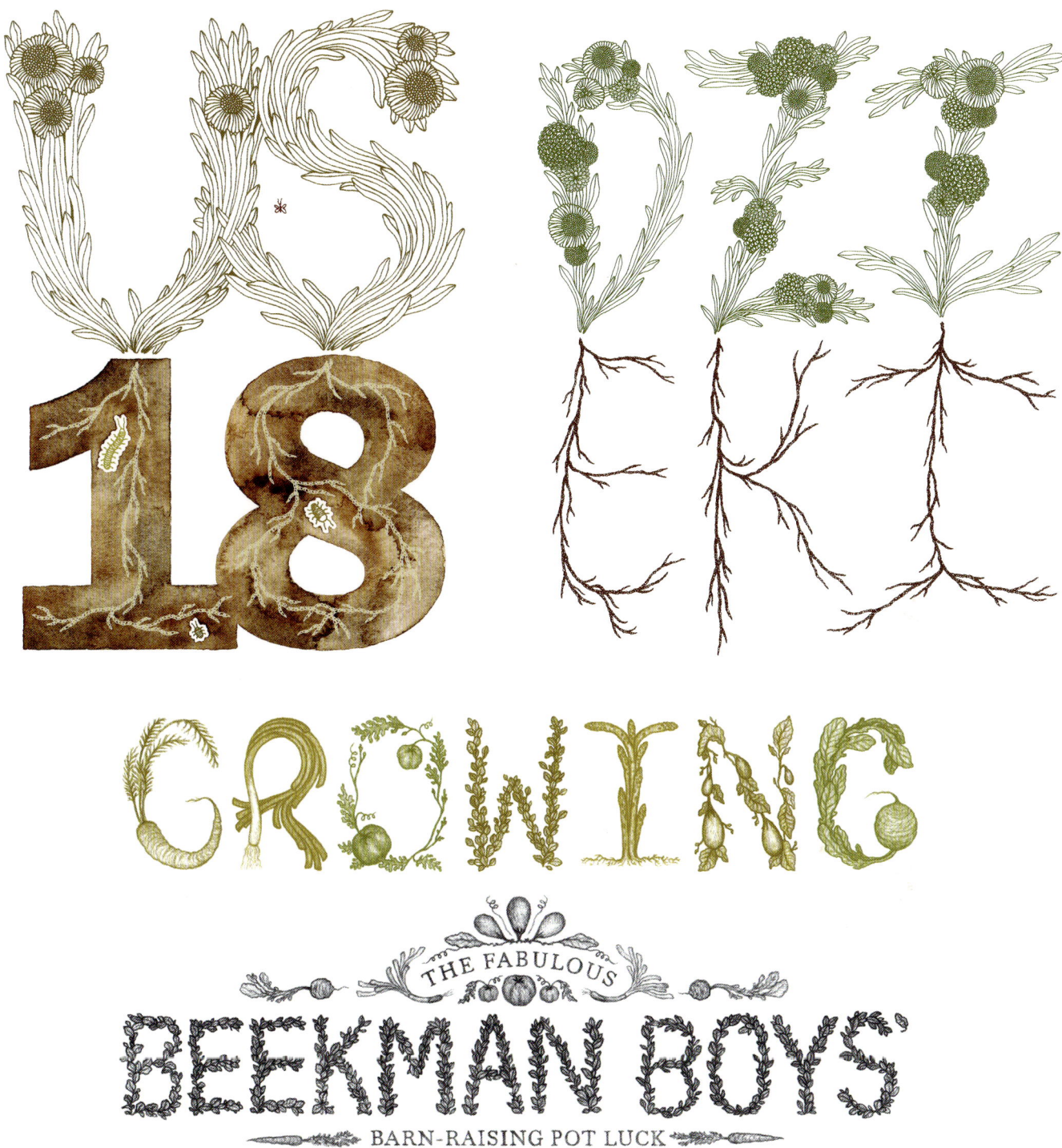

Organic US — Sasha Prood — Client: Verde Magazine

This typographic illustration was created in 2011 for Verde Magazine. It accompanied a feature on the dominance of organic framing in the USA compared to the rest of the world.

Dzieki — Sasha Prood — Art Director – Janek Swietlik — Client: Polish Humanitarian Action

This t-shirt illustration was created in 2011 as a pro bono project for the Scholz & Friends Warsaw agency. It was one of the six designs comprising a promotional campaign for the charitable organization Polish Humanitarian Action. The Polish word "Dzieki" translates to "thanks" in the charities slogan " People, thanks to whom the world becomes better".

Growing & Beekman Boys' — Sasha Prood — Art Director – Courtney Waddell — Client: Food & Wine Magazine

These typographic illustrations were created in 2011 for Food & Wine Magazines August issue. "Growing" was used as the title of the contents page and "Beekman Boys'" was used as the title of a feature describing a farming duo.

Spring/Summer 2011 Promotional Lettering   Sasha Prood

These two illustrations were created for self-promotion in spring/summer 2011. "Coming This Summer" was placed on the landing page of my soon-to-be-launched (at the time) web shop, the Print Shop. "Love Me Do" was printed on postcards and used as a self-promotional mailer.

Introducing The Print Shop Sasha Prood

This hand lettered email was created in 2011 for self promotion. It was developed as a way to introduce friends, family and bloggers to my newly-launched web shop, the Print Shop.

creature — Takashi Okada

Digital collage based on original drawing.

Death Takashi Okada

A2 drawing on pape.

Flor — Takashi Okada

A2 drawing on paper

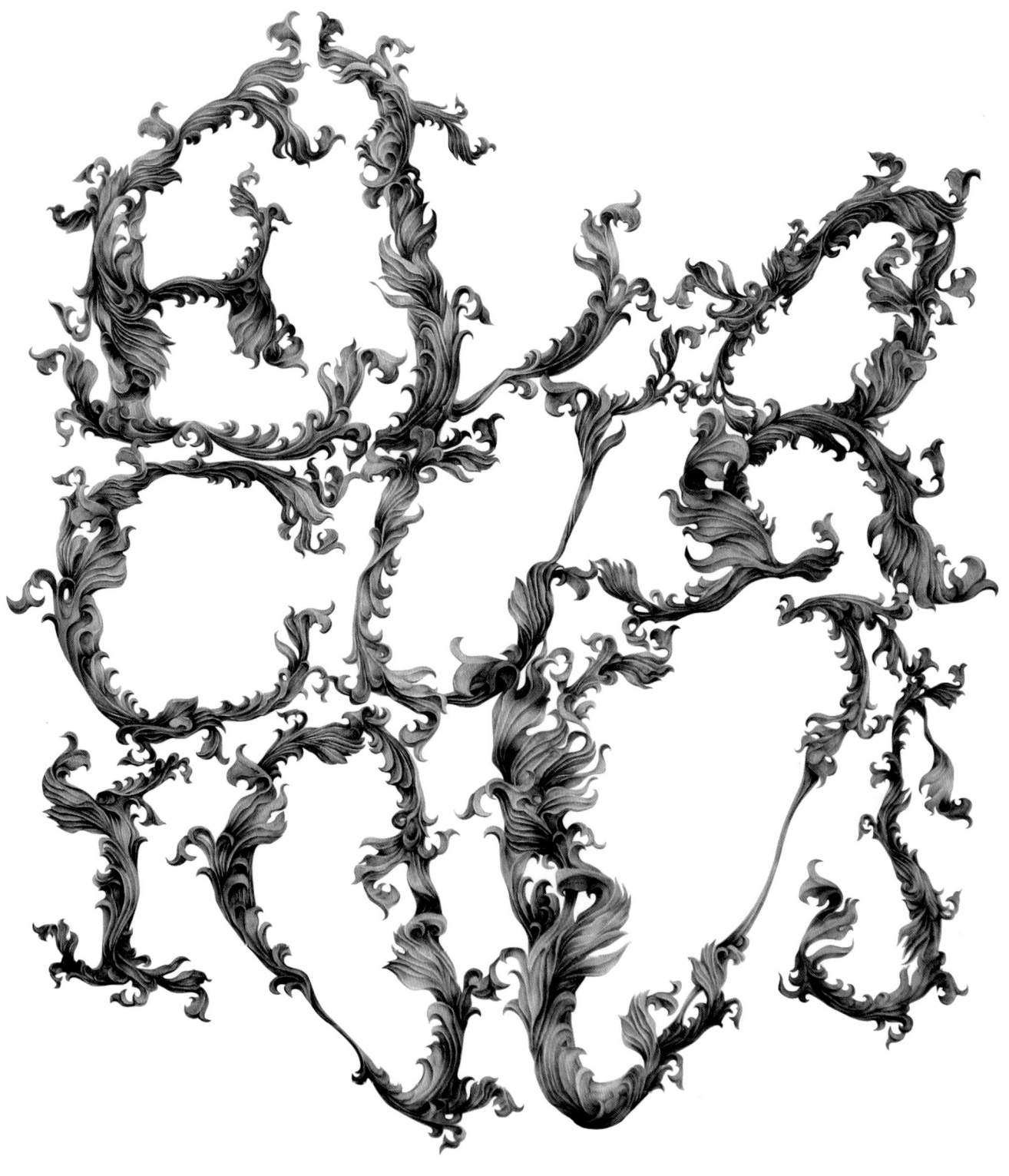

Elcurious — Takashi Okada

A2 drawing on pape.

Rebirth — Takashi Okada

A2 drawing on paper

Six Types — Takashi Okada

Flash exprimental motion/M13th Japan Media Arts Festival /Art Division Jury Recommend Works

Shortsqueeze — Takashi Okada — Client : shortsqueeze

Fashion ,select shop

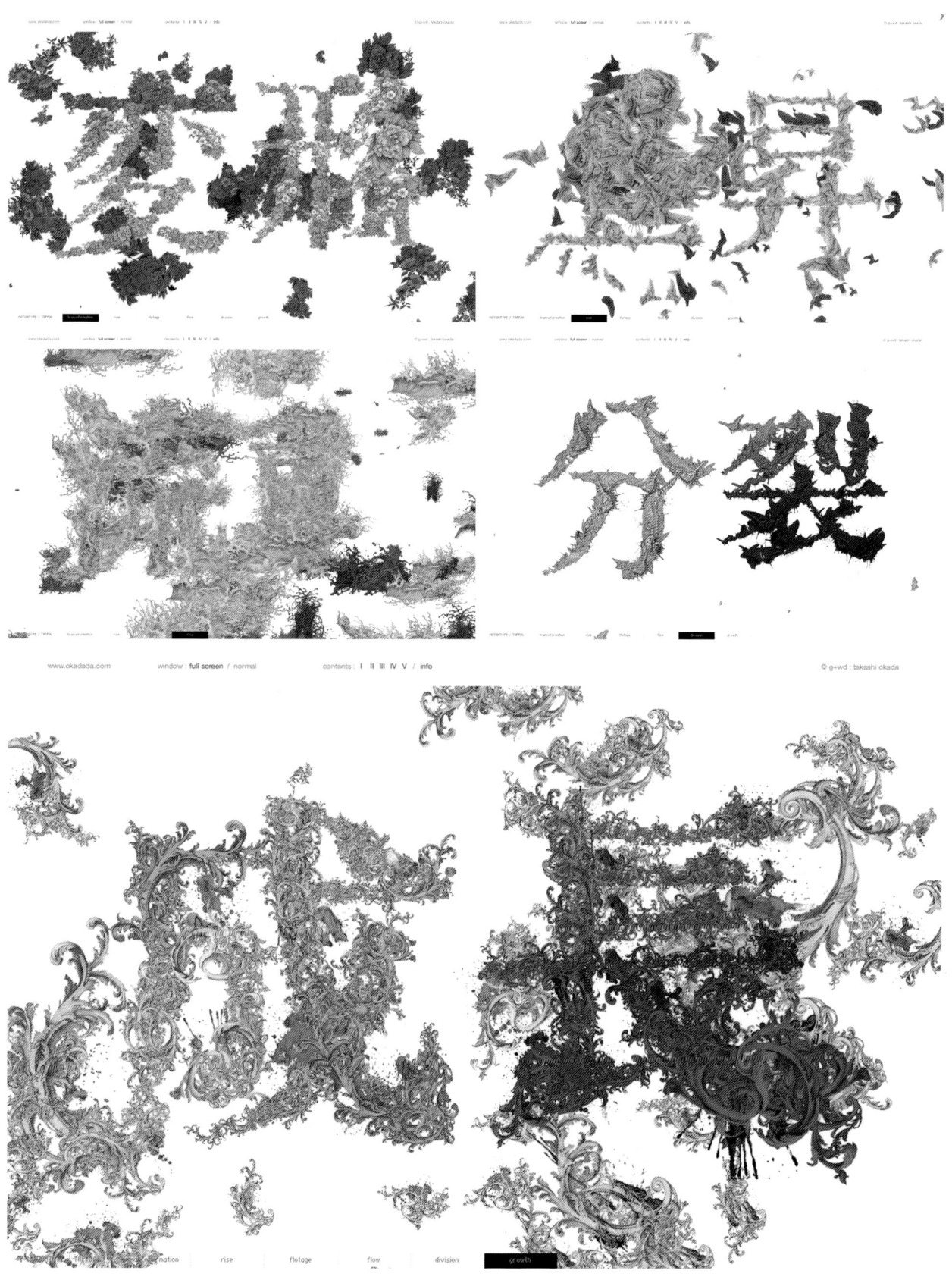

Trffdg — Takashi Okada

Flash exprimental motion/11th Japan Media Arts Festival /Art Division Jury Recommend Works.

&&&: Parts 1 and 2

Teagan White

Client/Created for: Gallery Nucleus; Illustrated Type Exhibit

Created for an illustrated type exhibition that showcased at Gallery Nucleus. The pieces are intended to hang an inch apart on the wall, the ends of the ampersands visually aligning to suggest eternity and the cycle of life and death.

Expand | Contract   Teagan White

This was a response to, and indirect attempt to communicate the feeling of, the real life experience of stumbling across animal bones in a field one evening. My boyfriend and i collected them (they were everywhere once we started paying attention) and I was able to draw those same bones from life in "Contract". Bones are odd things, brittle and fragile in places and unbreakable in others, always smaller than you expect them to be, and they feel and sound like toy blocks if they're knocked against each other

Converge | Depart

Teagan White

Continuation of a body of work dealing with life cycles. While creating this I was thinking about collective consciousness, and the possibility of an individual's consciousness being a partition of the whole, and would therefore in death be returned to a richer, more harmonious, more complete state. Not something I necessarily believe, but ideas are fun to play with.

Honey & Sorrow — Teagan White — Client: Amber Edgar

A lyric poster created for Amber Edgar's single, Honey & Sorrow. The bird and bee parallel her line, «song of the bird and sting of the bee, one goes sweetly, the other is teaching me how to move on».

Everything Is A Cycle Teagan White

An exploration of the concepts of life cycles and reciprocal arrangements between living things and the earth. I have a nearly religious reverence for decomposers, and the idea that the vehicle through which we achieve a very real (if only physical) immortality is the lowest of life forms, who go about their work indiscriminately and with no expectation of praise in return.

Inhale | Exhale — Teagan White

Examination of life cycles expressed through a life-death relationship. The text, Inhale and Exhale, is intended to imply that both life and death are temporary and cyclical, rather than a beginning and an end.

Only Skin — Teagan White — Client: Graeme McGregor

Typographic tattoo design based on the lyrics for the Joanna Newsom song 'Only Skin'

Set of Typography illustrations — Anton Gorbunov

I paint by hands, I like when picture looks like hand-drawn. Cos I love the inaccuracies and mistakes in any art. I think it shows the author. In spite of this I am inspired by the exact mathematical form, perfect lace in baroque style, the exact lines of graving style and typographical rhyme. I always pleased to go out on contact with interesting people, willing to participate in new projects.

Set of Typography illustrations
Anton Gorbunov

a picture is worth a thousand words   Juan Osborne

A picture being worth a thousand words... literally!

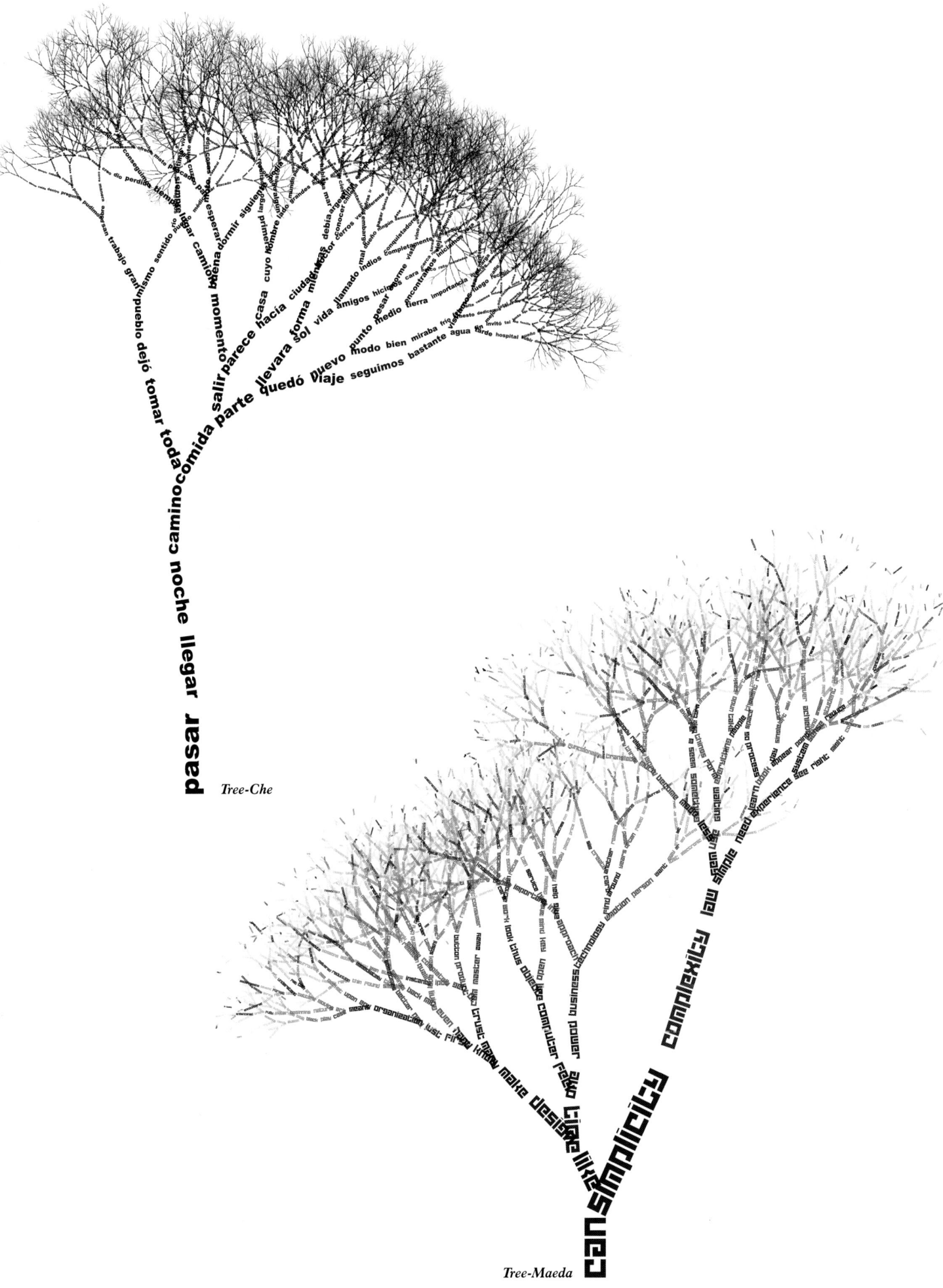

Tree-Che

Tree-Maeda

Daniela y el Mar

The Secret of Jules Verne - otra stopwords

Freud

122&123

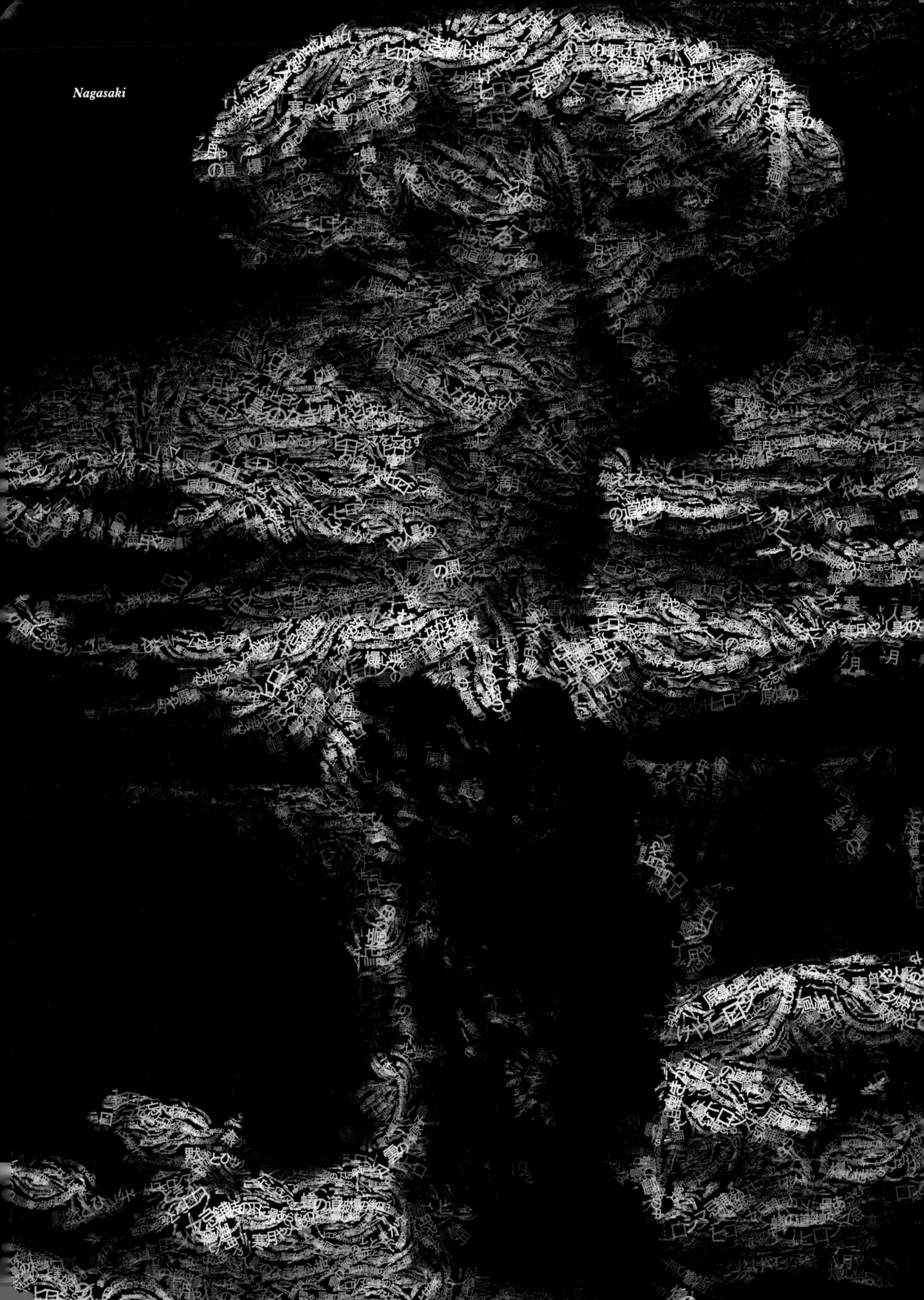

WordInPeace

JuanOsborne.com

124&125

189.429 words
New Testament

Hand of Man

The Bible
Words of the New and Old Testament

Villa

Villa=Gol!
David Villa Team Spain World Cup 2010

Lorca02

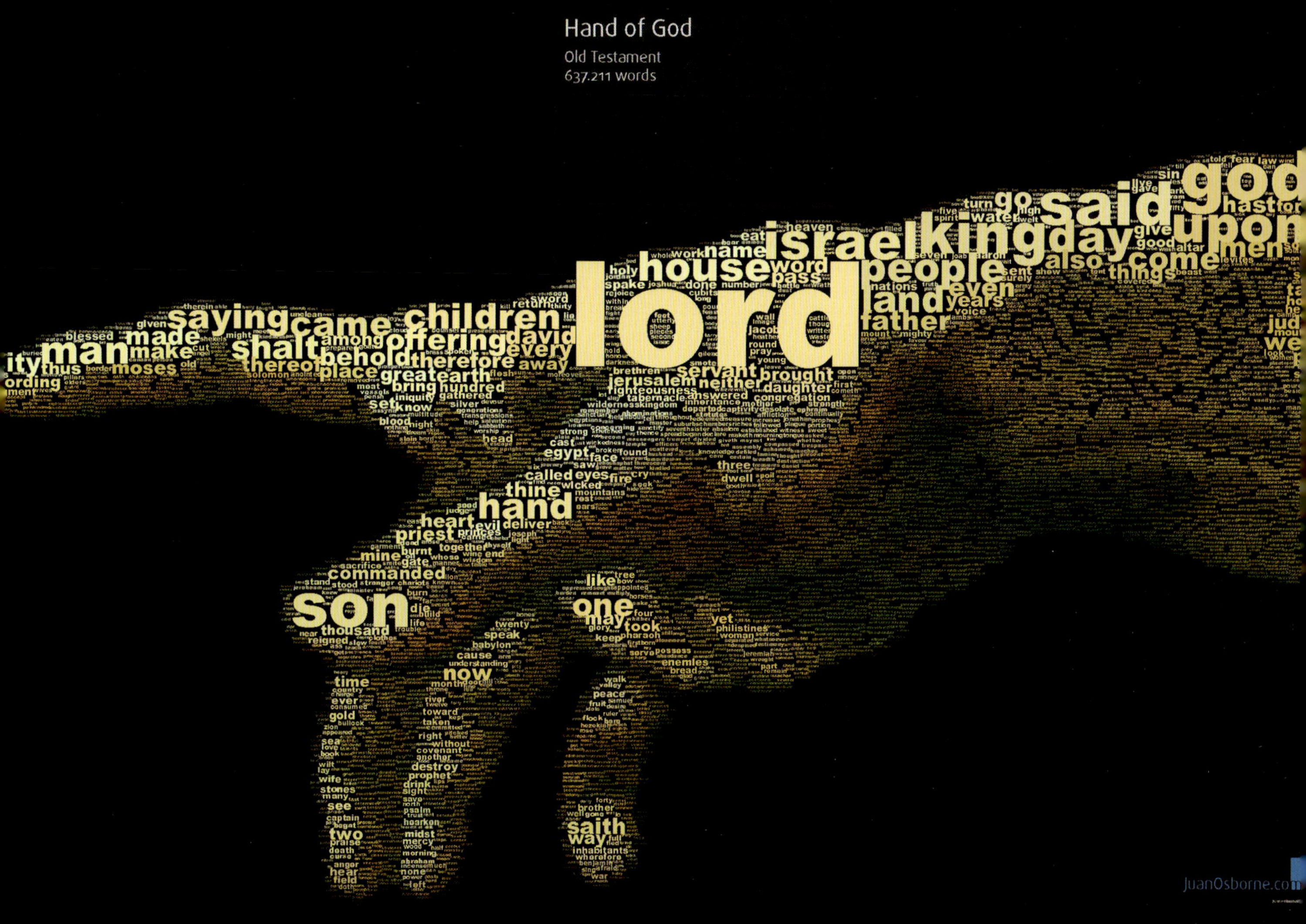

Hand of God
Old Testament
637.211 words

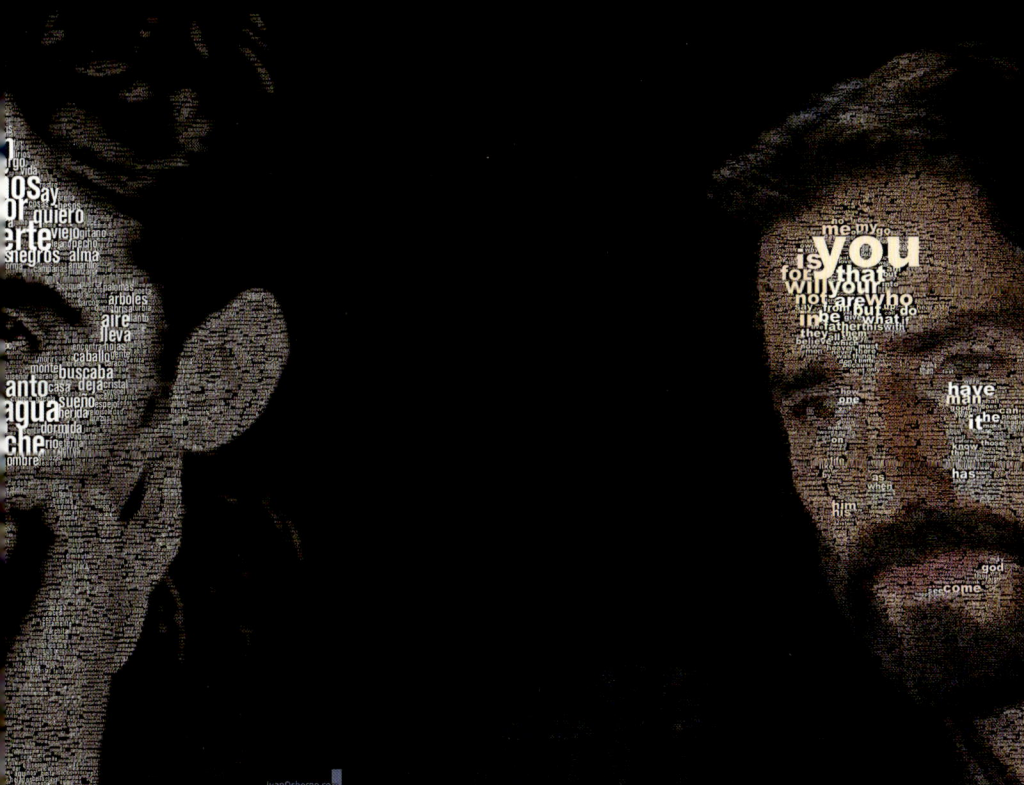

JesusWords01-ING

Flamenco

AMERICAN CANCER SOCIETY

Am I Collective

Client: THE MARTIN AGENCY, USA

Poster Illustration about smoke-free laws in America.

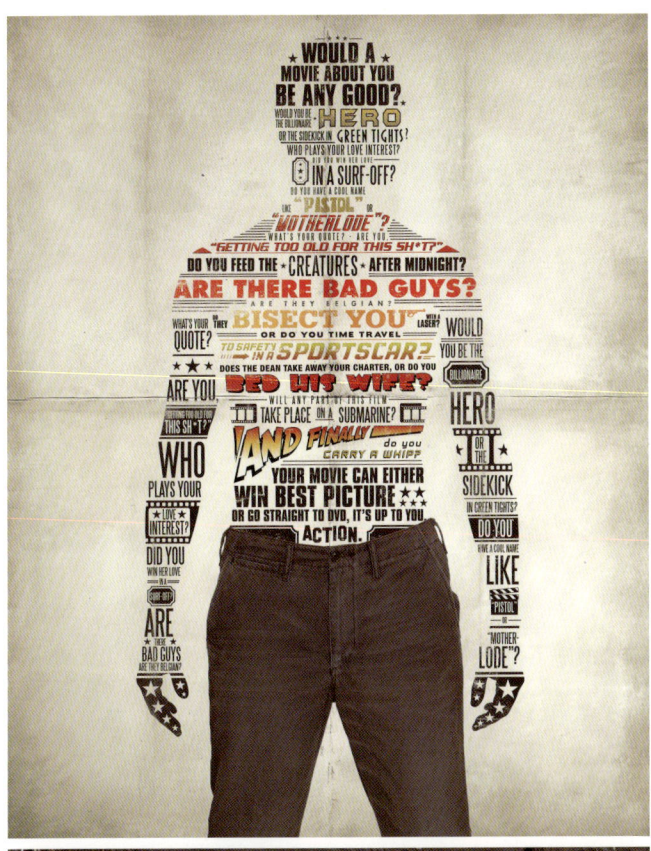

DOCKERS USA

Am I Collective

Client: DRAFT FCB, USA

Typographic posters promoting the brands latest range of cargo pants.

HELLO TO THE AMERICAS - PITCH Am I Collective Client: EMIRATES AIRLINES, NETHERLANDS

3D Typographic illustration that showcases all the destinations in the U.S one can travel to with Emirates Airlines.

LOWE BULL — Am I Collective — Client: LOWE BULL, S.A.

Typographic poster that represents the agency's values.

MINI   AM I COLLECTIVE   Client: BLACK RIVER F.C., JOHANNESBURG

Print ad using typography to depict how the shape of the mini has changed over the years.

S.A. DAIRY　　　　　　　　　　　　　Am I Collective　　　　　　　　　　　　　Client: FOX P2

Typographic treatment for the Dairy Association of South Africa for print ads.

VODAFONE — Am I Collective — Client: YELLOW BRANDS, AUSTRALIA

Typographic poster that represents the agency's values.

Suppport Japan — André Beato — Client: Wall for Japan

Illustration designed for WALL FOR JAPAN cause, Wallpaper created to App for iPhone and iPad

Lisbonlovers — André Beato — Client: Lisbonlovers

Illustration created for the Lisbonlovers manifesto

Friends of Type — André Beato

Illustration created for Friends of Type blog

Honor and Pride — André Beato — Client: KDU

Illustration created for the KDU X Idn book

Don´t Sweat My Swag — André Beato — Client: Nike
Design for Nike

Barcelona — André Beato — Client: NEUE
Illustration created for NEUE Magazine; Show Us Your Type Issue 2 | Barcelona

Swagger Back — André Beato
Typographic Experience

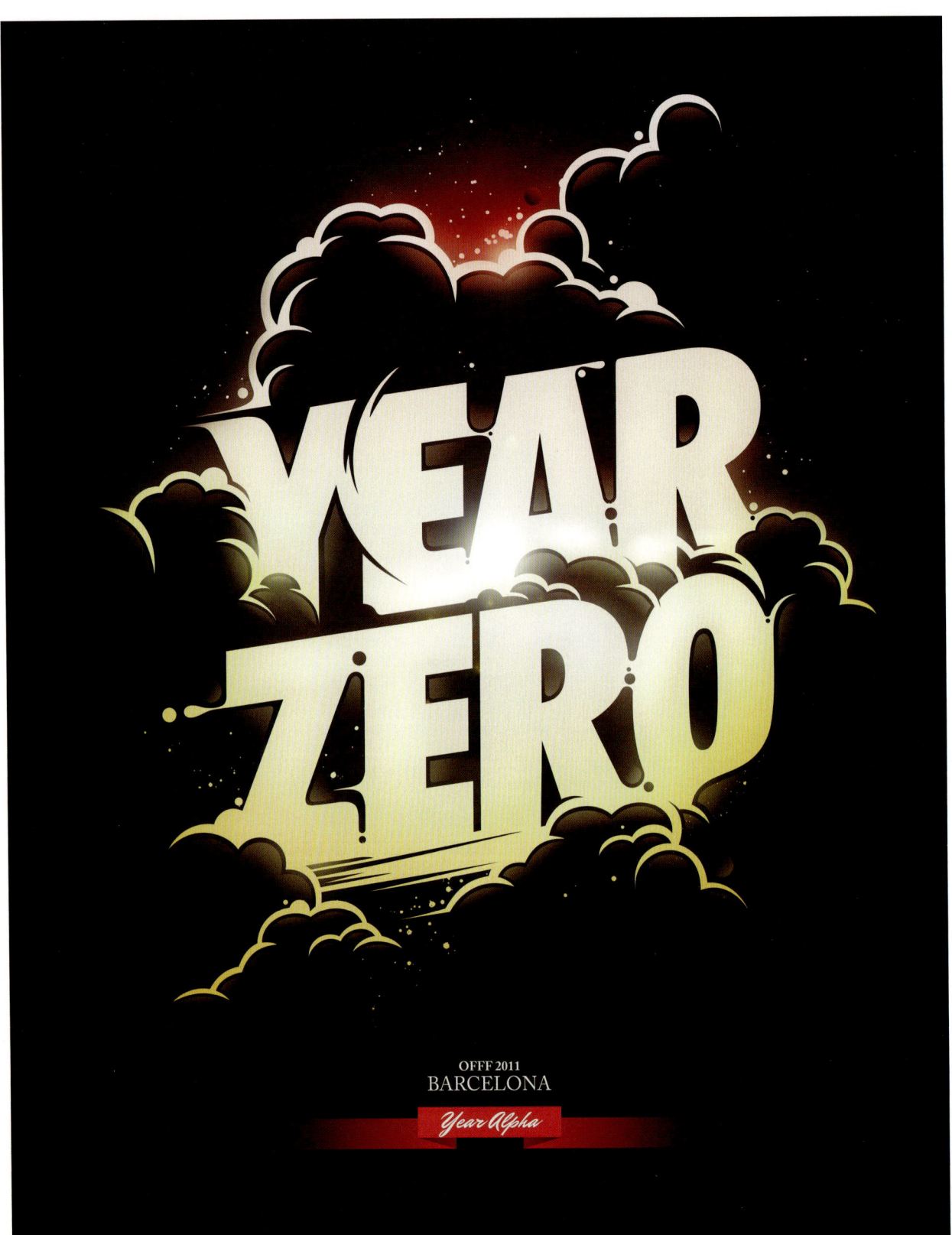

Honor and Pride

André Beato

Client: OFFF

Illustration created for the OFFF 2011 catalogue

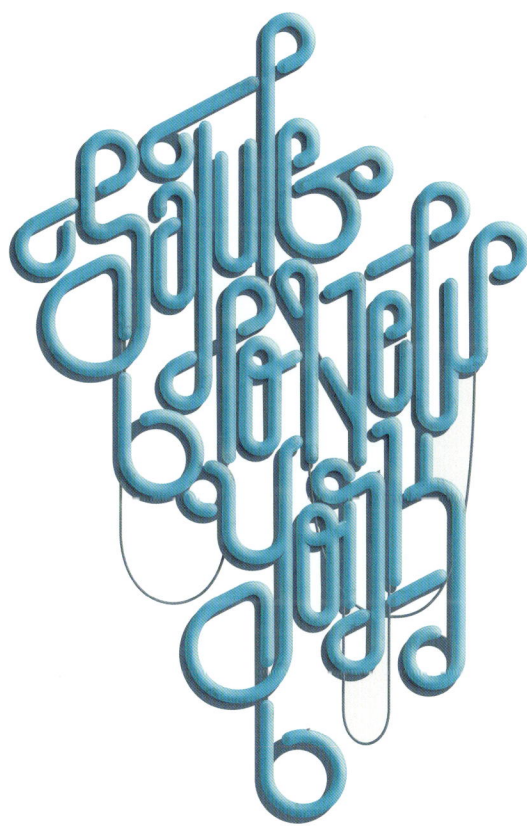 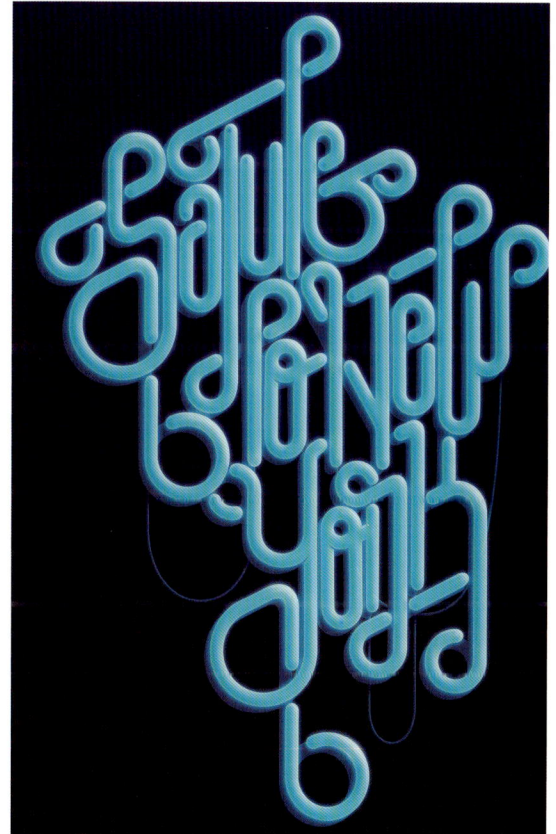

Oh La La! — André Beato

Illustration created for the from Paris Collective

Salute to New York — André Beato

Illustration based on Tony Forster design Salute

Sumol Lisboa André Beato Client: Sumol X Lisbonlovers

Merchandising Graphic Proposal Sumol X Lisbonlovers Project

Unknown Disorder — André Beato — Client: OFFF

Illustration created for the OFFF 2011 catalogue

Demons of Seduction

BLANQ

Designer: WaWa Ho & Eddie Teng
Jeffrey Wang & Caroline Yang
Photographer: Liang Su

Sculpture of temptation, craft of sensation.
body of a woman - Crazy Horse Paris whispers - is allure.
Intriguing lines, ethereal figures.
Feline souls in literary classics – BLANQ imagines - are beauty.
With the Crazy Horse Paris, seduction is a journey. Driven by the god-forbidden yet primitive desire, another step forward is another step towards beautiful risque. Danger silently crawls behind enchantments in disguise, luring you to step closer and closer. The illusion of temptation is a sweet wrap of pain. The bittersweet of struggle and crave.
Travel east to the Journey to the West, a classic Chinese folktale about the legendary primilage to India of Buddhist saints. Before achieving the epic mission, the heroes have to win a sensational combat declared by picturesque demons. The femme fatales enslave men with their fatally ethereal talents. Every slightest gesture smokes lust. Every sweetest smile melts morality. Every alluring movement is an irresistible call for your heart and soul. Their beauties, their very different soft powers are the best art of seduction.
Be the prey of these decadent but divine. Here, now.

【白骨精：千面幻化】
THE BONE

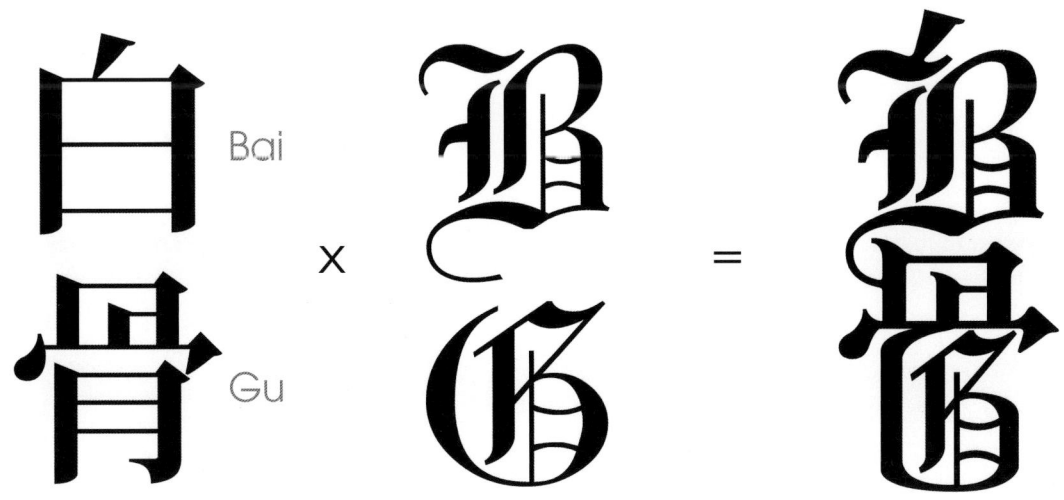

【蜘蛛精：工於心計】
THE SPIDER

蜘 Jhih × ʃ = 蜘
蛛 Jhu   ʃ   蛛

【狐狸精：誘之以情】
THE FOX

狐狸 (Hu Li) × HL = 狐狸

【鐵扇公主：熾熱掌控】
IRON MAIDEN

鉄 Tie × T = 铁
扇 Shan   S   扇

1. 99 problems

2. Allow Things to Happen

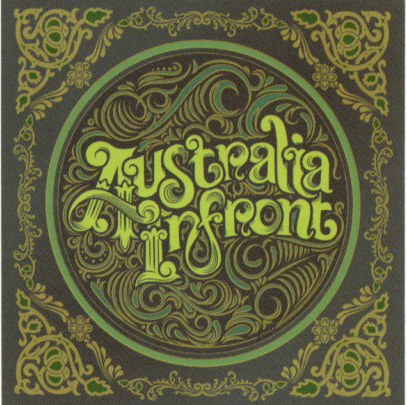

3. Australia Infront

1. 99 problems *2. Allow Things to Happen* *3. Australia Infront* *4. Bobby wallpaper iphone*
5. Bohemian Rhapsody *6. Born to be wild* *7. (avatar project) cara wallpaper* *8. Australian*
9. Dreams are meant to be lived *10. Hell Hath No Fury* *11. Think Creative think different*
12. Jibriel *13. Sybilla* *14. Historiaster*

Bobby Haiqalsyah

Clients: Nosta, The Deadwords project (Karen To), Jibriel, Sybilla band, Dewalio, Australian Infront , Nosta, MNC promo

Various typographic works between 2011-2012 some are personal projects (1,3,10,12) and other are client works or pitches over the two years. Some of these typographic work and experiments started from his avatar project (4&7) where we take a name and create a typographic piece based on those names. It became a regular commission after sometime to do these pieces, but in most cases the clients wishes to have a similar style to the preceding two designs (4&7). The demand led to projects similar to it in my office (11) where I got to do more of these typographic experiment using letters as image.

I kept pursuing this world of typography with passion and gravitating towards the artist that influenced my work such as Luca Ionescu and Andre Beato. I later realised that they too had influences from past masters in type and lettering. Thus I dove deeper into the world of type and lettering and found a friendly and open community of peers that accepts my work but also a whole history of different people from different cultures who does this craft for a living and doing them exceptionally.

My research and exploration has since turned to some projects with clothing brands (2,6,9) which allowed more exploration and development. I keep exploring the possibility with type through client works, competition , and personal projects (10) and I hope to continue working on this vast world of type and lettering.

4. Bobby wallpaper iphone

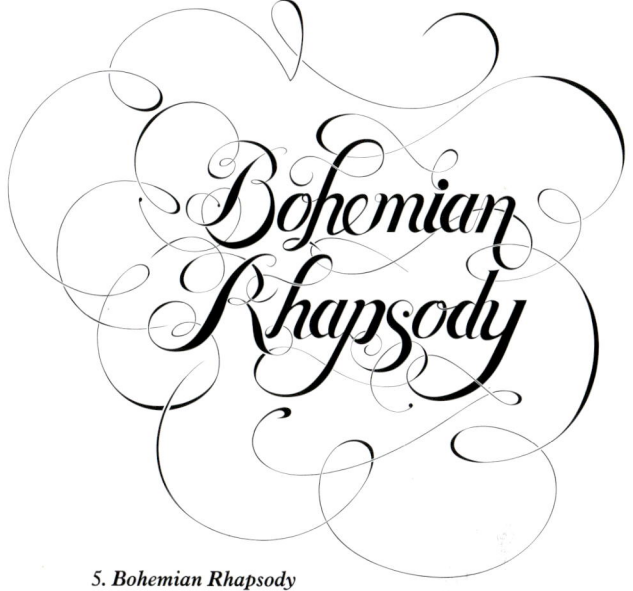

5. Bohemian Rhapsody

6. Born to be wild

7. (avatar project) cara wallpaper

8. Australian

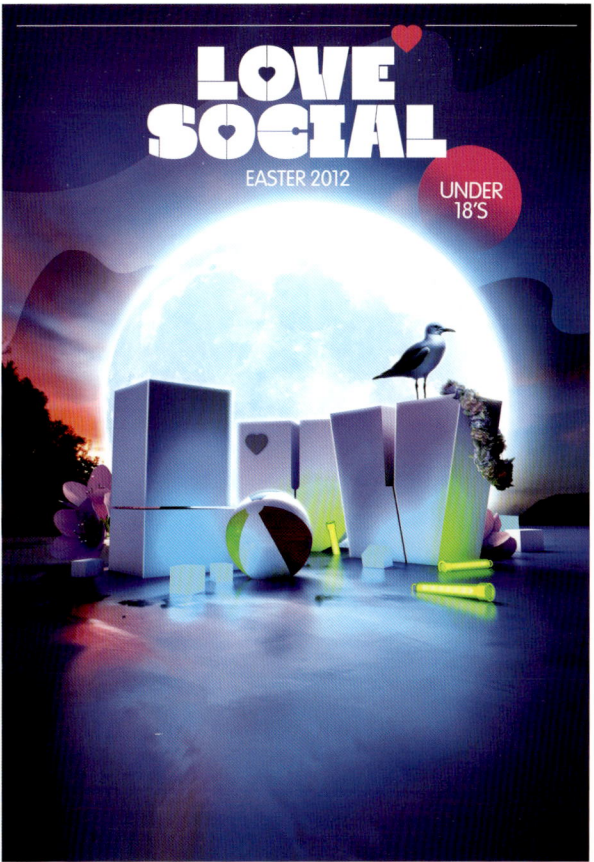

Love social   Brian Dixon   Design Agency: UYR Group
Creative Director: Fluid Design
Client: Luminar

Branded artwork for a regular under 18's clubbing event held at various nightclubs in the UK.

Vibe — Brian Dixon — Design Agency: UYR Group
Client: Luminar

Rebrand of a popular music event held in the UK. The logo was rendered in 3D and distorted slightly to create a futuristic look. The lighting was dimmed to give a sense of mystery and intrigue.

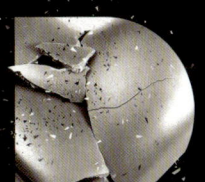

Fridays / 11pm - 4am
House, Techno, Dub-Step
£4 NUS / £6 on the door.

Fridays / 11pm - 4am
House, Techno, Dub-Step
£4 NUS / £6 on the door.

Fridays / 11pm - 4am
House, Techno, Dub-Step
£4 NUS / £6 on the door.

Circus — Brian Dixon — Design Agency: UYR Group / Client: Luminar

Teaser for a Circus themed night. The client requested that the imagery should be dark and sinister with a vintage feel.

Damaged — Brian Dixon — Design Agency: UYR Group / Client: Luminar

Branded artwork for a regular dance music event.
Each month, the letter D of the logo is cracked, smashed, warped, frayed, and damaged.
With the D centered in the middle, white on black, the aim is to create a recognizable brand regardless of how damaged it really is.

POP-TYPE

Brian Dixon

Design Agency: UYR Group
Client: Luminar

Personal project.
An abstract font created using basic colors and simple geometric shapes.

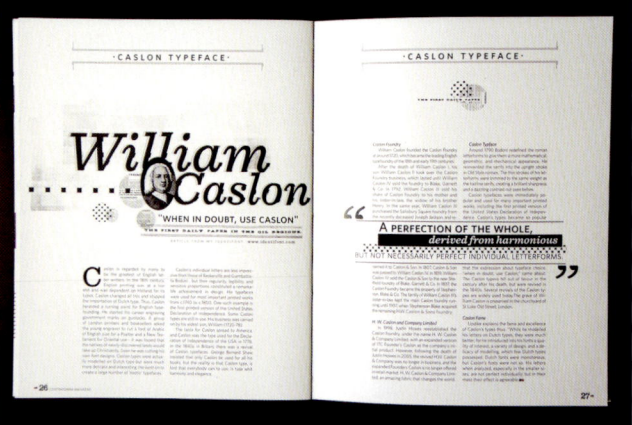

Contraforma Magazine Camila Montejo

Experimental and Typography magazine, using different kindsof typography.

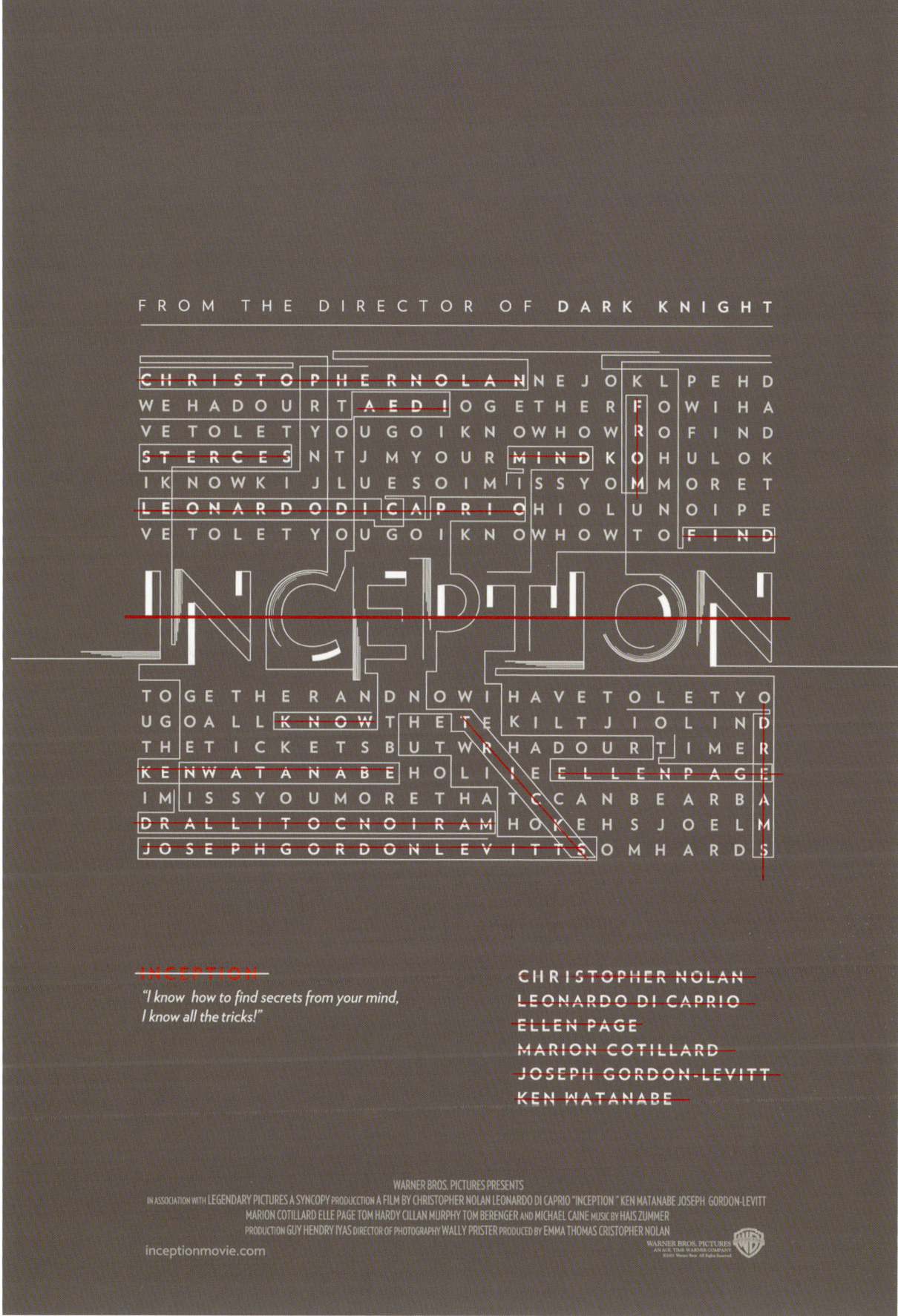

Inception Poster Camila Montejo

Free adaptation of the poster's design from the movie of Christopher Noan "Inception" taken into account the composition and digraming rules (Simetry- Regularity – Passivity – Unity- Accent, among others.) Academic Project.

Barranquilla Poster — Camila Montejo

Creating a Typography poster about a famous carnaval in Colombia, "El Carnaval de Barranquilla"

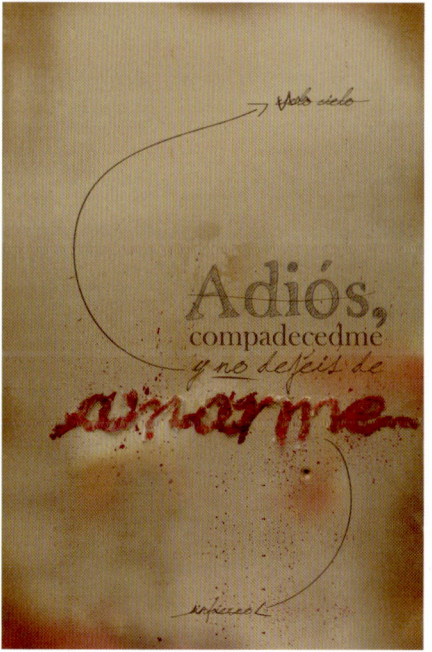

Marques de Sade Postcards — Camila Montejo

Student proyect inspired by a famous author "Marques de Sade
Serial of 10 postcards for Typography Module.
Development of postcards quoting well-know Marquis de Sade, showing the author's escence.

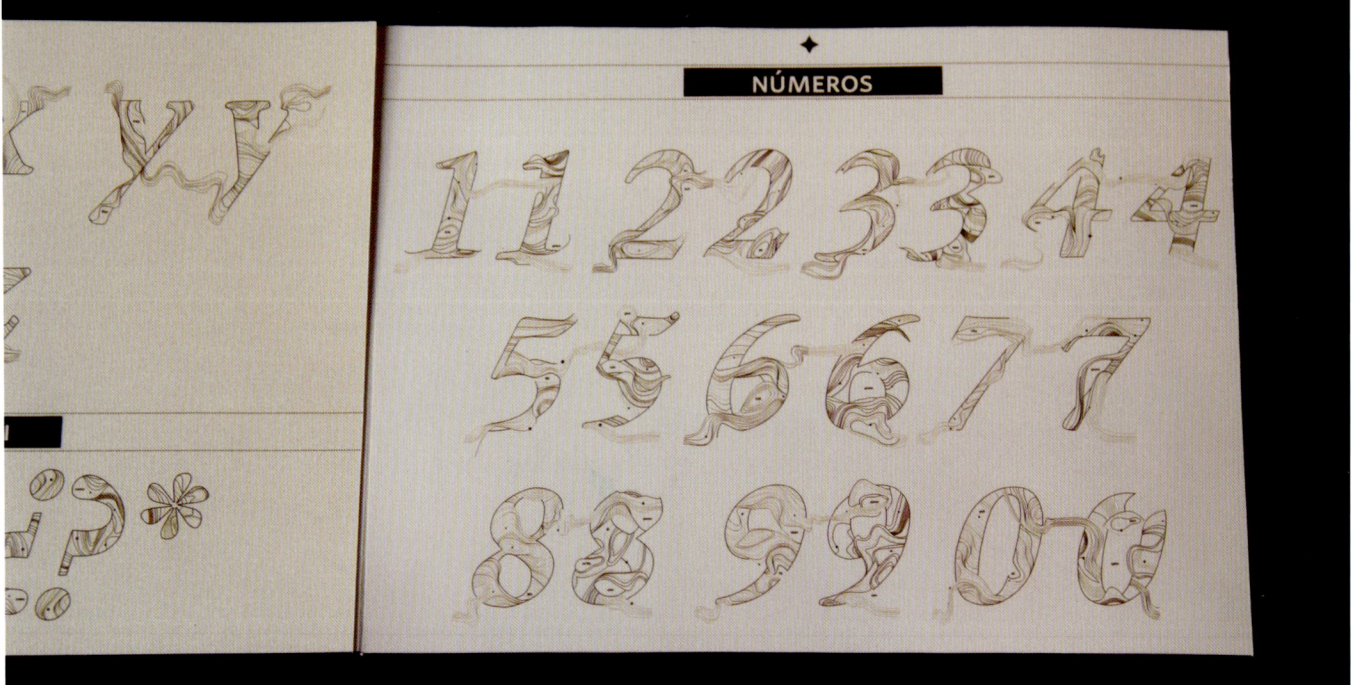

Topography Rocks — Camila Montejo and Catalina D'Amato — Photographer: Manuela Garces and Monica González

Typography creation from Topography, Cartography and Oceanography. The typography is called "Topography Rocks" it has the alphabeth from A to Z.

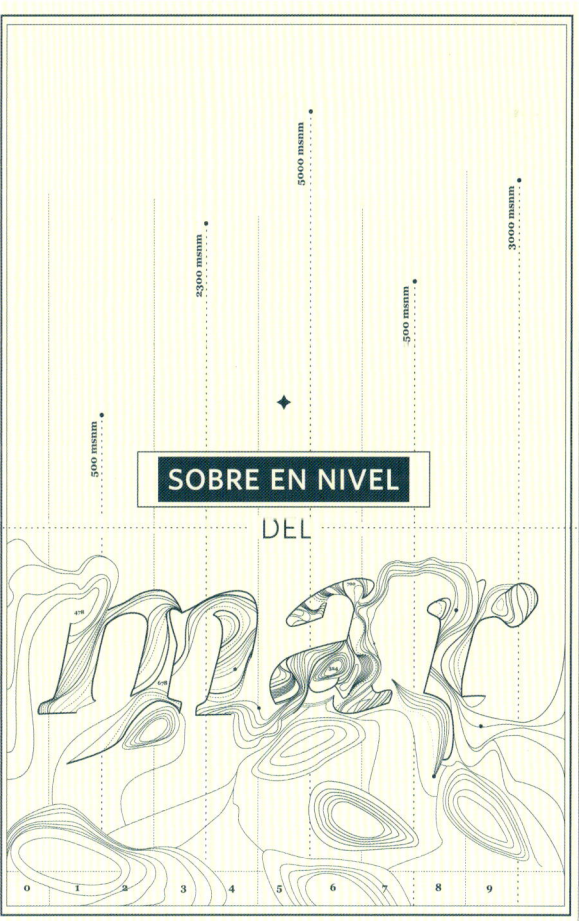

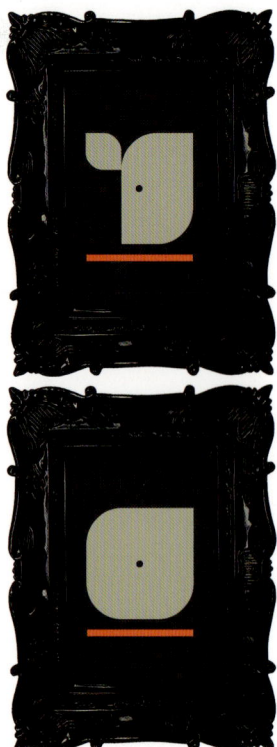
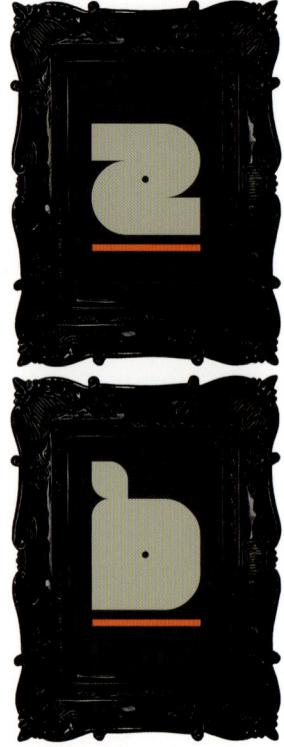
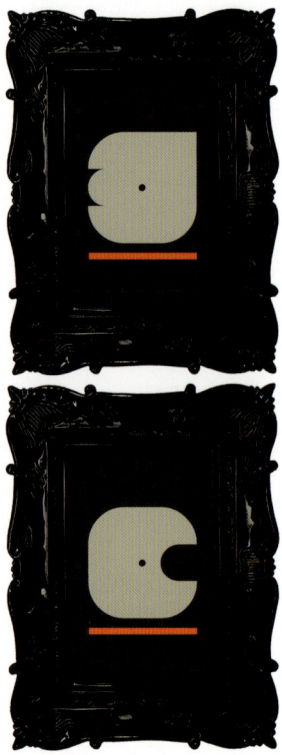

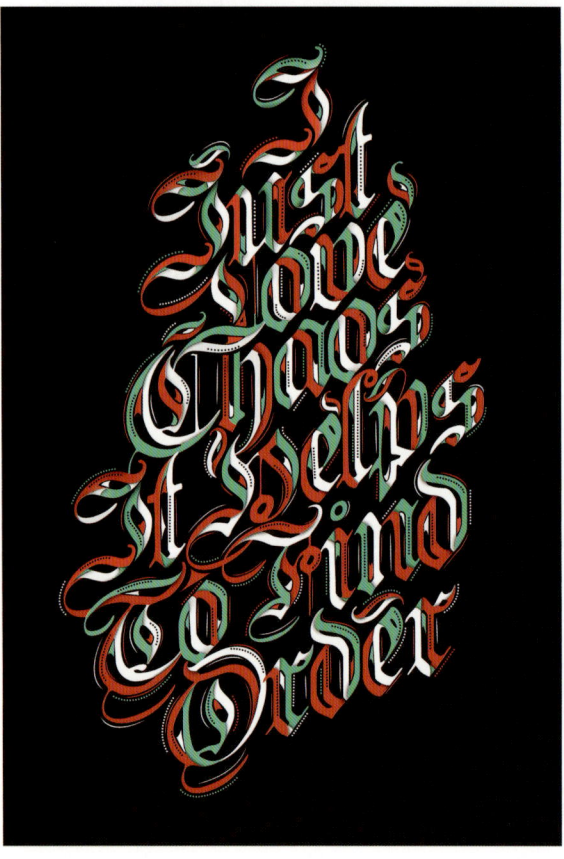

01.base typeface   Fabian de Lange

Free decorative bold font the mission was to create a "fat" bold font with lots of personality and charisma, We are glad to tell you that the download number reaches already more than 100.000!

Chaos   Fabian de Lange

"i just love chaos, it helps to find order"

Well done Fabian de Lange

Quik type play, july 2012 A growing collection of typographic experiments

Clean up Fabian de Lange

Quik type play, A growing collection of typographic experiments

So, Let there be type Fabian de Lange

Personal Type Experiment

Unknown   Fabian de Lange

Type illustration. Unknown dissorder, Each OFFF edition they published a book/cataloguewith artworks from all featured artists.This book will include texts, artworks and movies.

Back to Black   Fabian de Lange

Back to Black is a decorative typeface, The readability is perhaps less in the foreground,Thats why it also named back to black,I think black stands for simple clean and elegant, everythink what this typeface dont't have

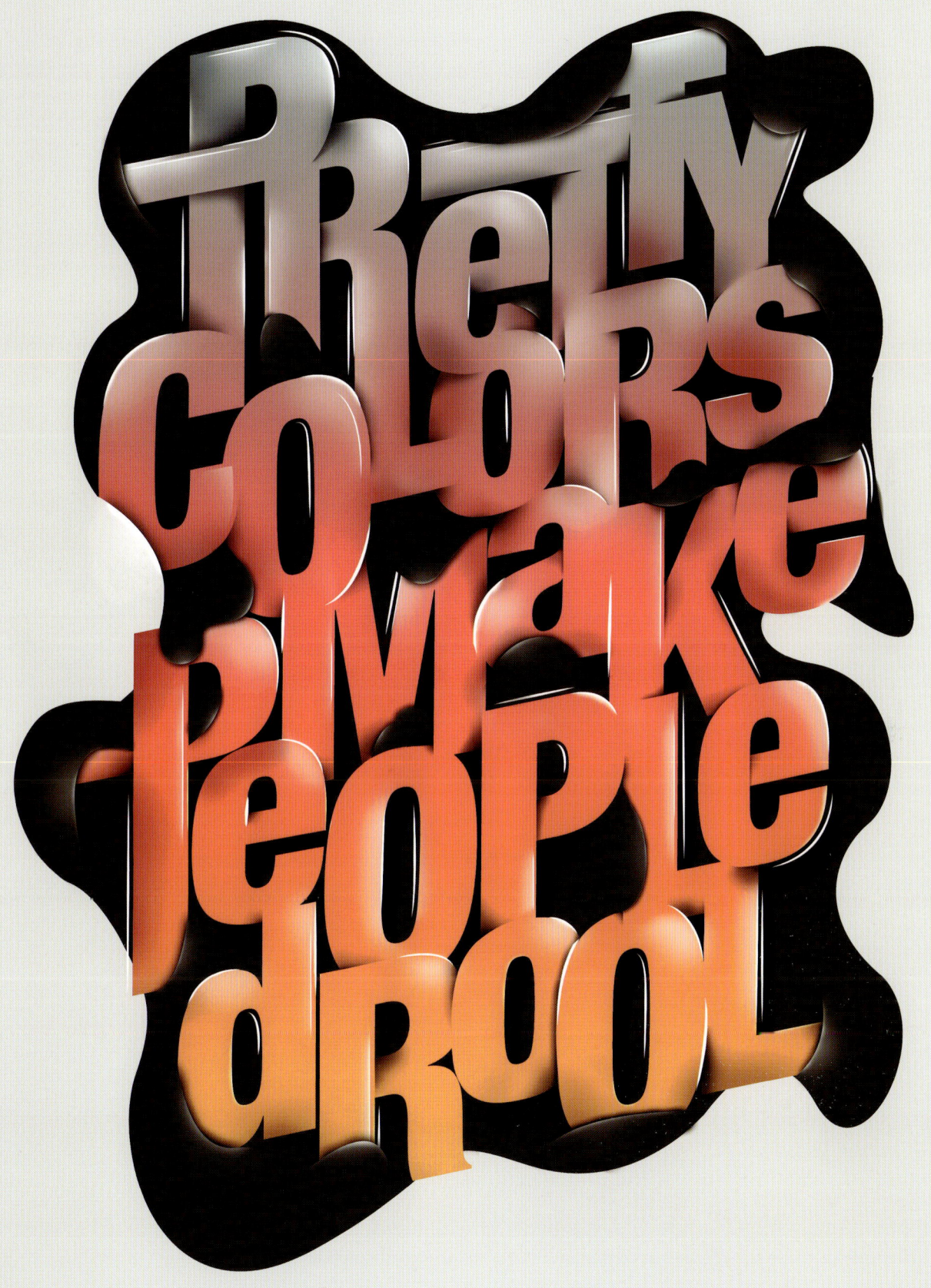

Drool — Fabian de Lange

Type Experiment "pretty colors make people drool"

Dacs

Fabian de Lange

Client: DACS united

Designers Against Child Slavery is a design collective thatenables creatives from all over the world to rise up against sex tradeThe name of the DACS exhibition is "Episodes".This exhibition is all about telling the story of a trafficking victim, through our artworkThe exhibition was showing live in New York City, in October.

Good time

Fabian de Lange

Experiment, and also soon available as skateboard deck

Fli Fest Götz Gramlich

Multiplied, constructed letters for a multidisciplinary arts festivals.
Selected for a Certificate of Typographic Excellence, TDC New York.

HerbstZeitLose — Götz Gramlich

Sikscreen Poster for a multidisciplinary Arts Festival in Heidelberg. The Herbstzeitlose is also a flower which combines, in a graphical way, these disciplines.
Selected for the Tokyo TDC Annual 2012.
Selected for a Certificate of Typographic Excellence, TDC New York.
Selected for the 23th International Poster Biennale Warsaw.
Selected for Golden Bee 12 - Moscow International Biennale of Graphic Design.

Unwörter & -sinn — Götz Gramlich

Poster for an exhibition with illustrated german faux-pas words and lyrics.

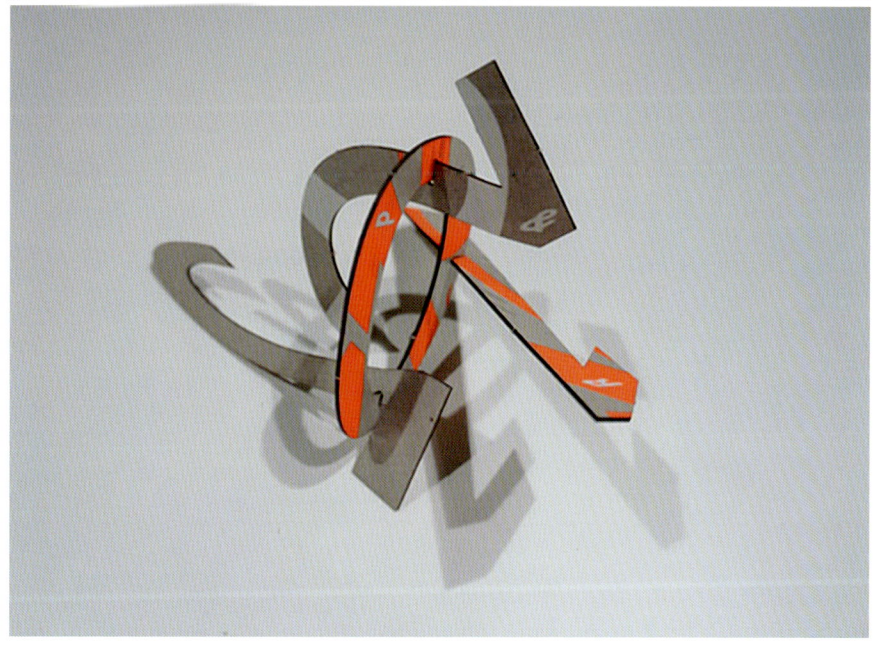

White Light

Hugo & Marie

Illustrator: Deanne Cheuk
Client: AIGA

Typographic poster created for the AIGA NY.

Don't Forget The Night   Hugo & Marie   Illustrator: Jules Julien
Client: Personal, created for Pick Me Up show in London.

Typographic poster created for London's annual contemporary graphic arts fair, Pick Me Up.

Cushnie et Ochs Print Hugo & Marie Illustrator: Mario Hugo
Client: Cushnie et Ochs

Print created for Cushnie et Ochs FW10 collection.

Charles Hugo & Marie Illustrator: Mario Hugo
Client: Spin Studios

Drug-related illustrations created for Channel 4's anniversary book. The illustrated quotes are filled with hidden contextual narratives.

Robin — Hugo & Marie — Illustrator: Mario Hugo — Client: Spin Studios

Drug-related illustrations created for Channel 4's anniversary book. The illustrated quotes are filled with hidden contextual narratives.

Hanne Hukkelberg   Hugo & Marie   Illustrator: Mario Hugo
                                                                                                            Client: Non-Format

Illustrated type treatment and illustration for Hanne Hukkelberg. Design by Non-Format.

Beck, Modern Guilt   Hugo & Marie   Illustrator: Mario Hugo
                                                                                       Client: Capitol Records

Conceptual album packaging for Beck Modern Guilt. Created for Interscope Records.

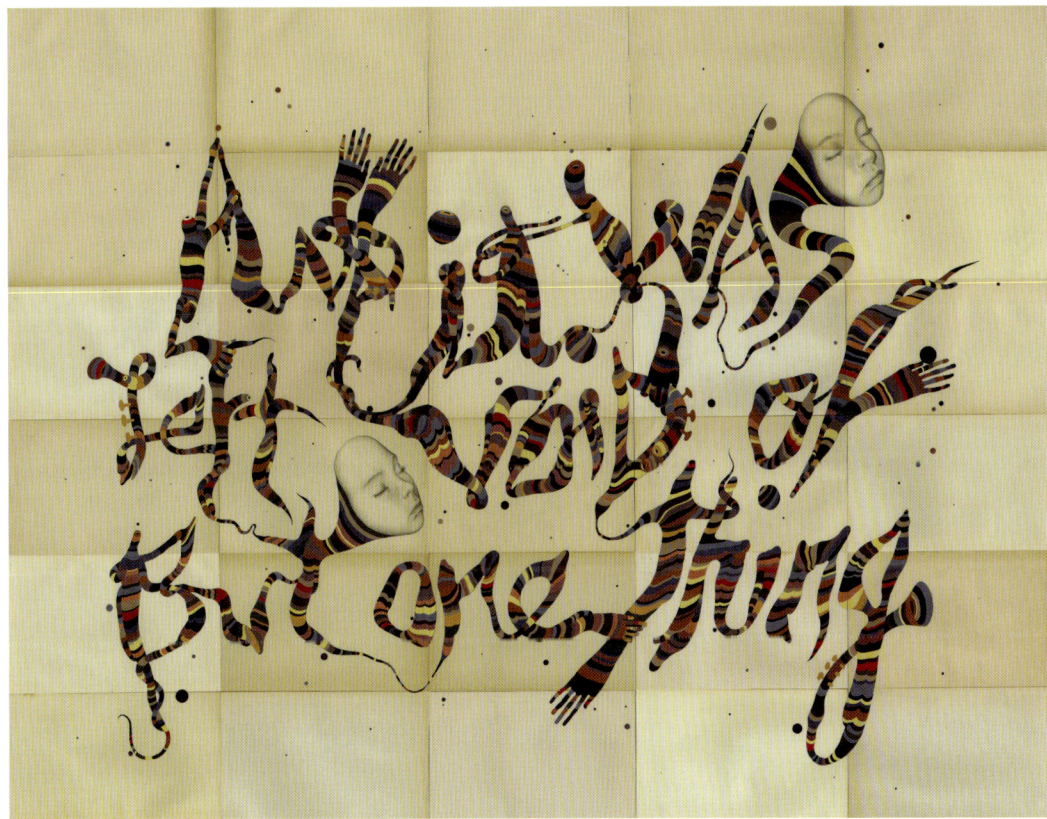

Inspiration — Hugo & Marie — Illustrator: Mario Hugo — Client: Microsoft

One of a typographic poster series created for Microsoft.

La Surprise — Hugo & Marie — Illustrator: Mario Hugo — Client: Studio La Surprise

Type treatment celebrating the opening of new Parisian studio, La Surprise.

And it Was Left Void — Hugo & Marie — Illustrator: Mario Hugo — Personal piece

Personal illustration created for solo show at Vallery Vasava gallery in Barcelona.

92nd Street Y | Hugo & Marie | Illustrator: Mike Perry
Client: 92nd Street YMCA

Campaign illustration created for the 92nd street Y.

The Fader X (RED) | Hugo & Marie | Illustrator: Micah Lidberg
Client: The Fader Magazine

Aids Free in 2013 for (RED) and The Fader Magazine.

TDC Type Poster

Hugo & Marie

Illustrator: Mario
Client: Type Directors Club, New York Chapter

Typographic poster created for the Type Director's Club Posters of Fortune benefit project

Bad typography   Igor Mustaev

Lettering for «Living Letters» art-project.

Como Swing Crash Festival Logo   Igor Mustaev   Client: Como Swing Crash Festival

Logo for one of the most popular swing dance festival in Como (Italy).

Hot Stomp poster Igor Mustaev

Lettering for «Living Letters» art-project.

Identity for Swing Dance Couple   Igor Mustaev   Client: Igor Pavlov & Marina Alekseeva

Identity for one of the most popular swing dance couple in Moscow (Russia).

Months of the year　　　　　　　　　　Igor Mustaev

Lettering for postcards.

1.Kit Out Your Studio

2.Location, Location, Location

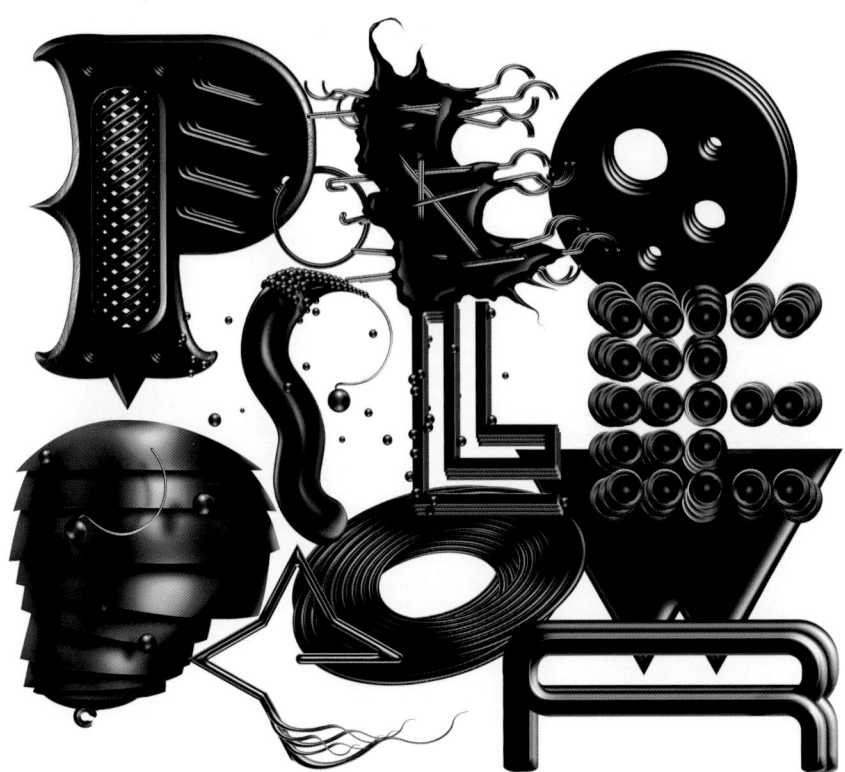

3.People Power

1.Kit Out Your Studio	*2.Location, Location, Location*	*3.People Power*	István Szugyiczky	Client: Computer Arts / UK
4.Promotions&Marketing	*5.Start Your Own Studio*			

Illustrative title lettering for a 5-part series of articles on how to start a design studio.

4.Promotions&Marketing

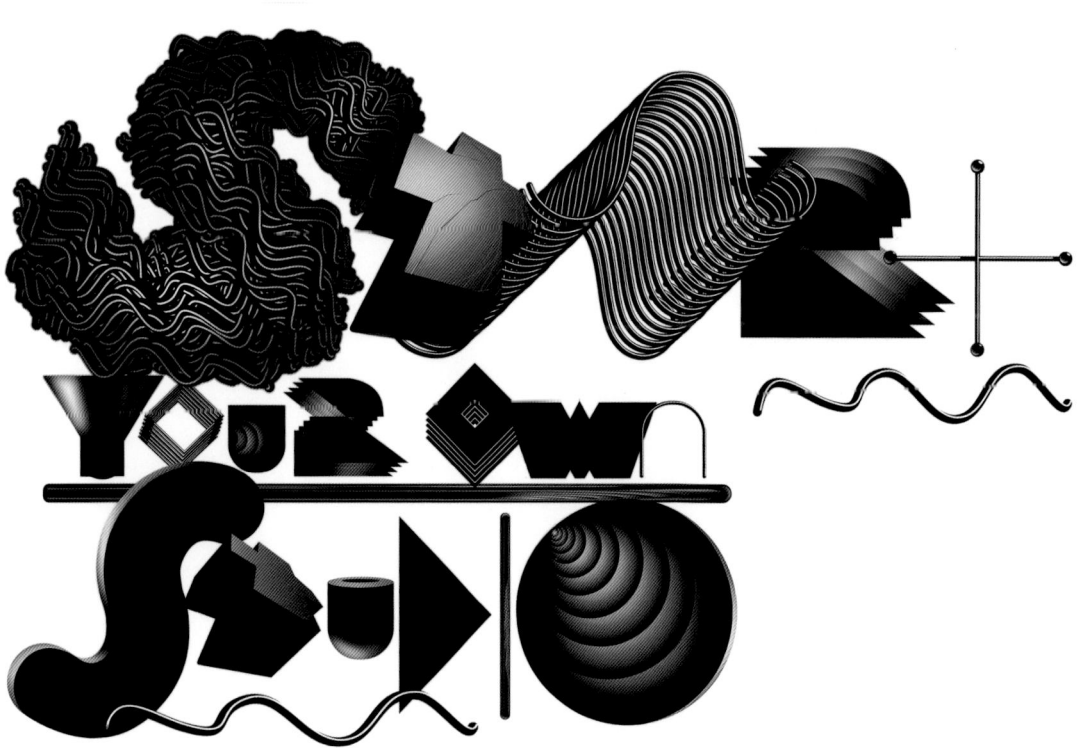

5.Start Your Own Studio

1.Love / Hate

2.'M' is for 'Morose

| *1.Love / Hate* | *2.'M' is for 'Morose* | *3.No Relation* | István Szugyiczky | Client: XENO.WS |
| *4.Quantum* | *5.Retrospectivo* | *6.Borderline* | | |

Print and T-shirt design for Xeno.ws

3.No Relation

4.Quantum

5.Retrospectivo

6.Borderline

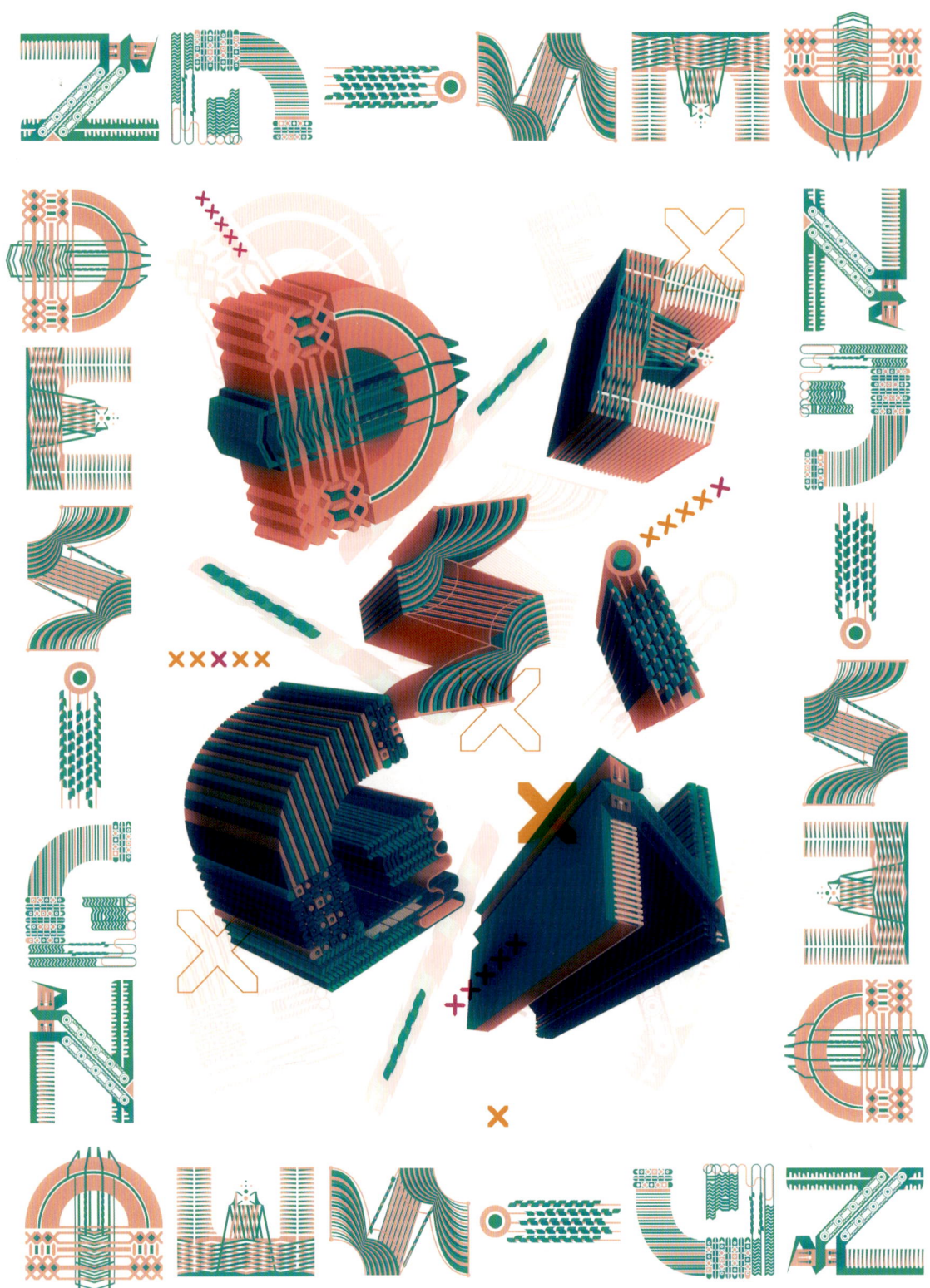

D-E-S-I-G-N Jorrit van Rijt

Illustrative character design of the word DESIGN. All together combined in a poster in which the characters are evolving in 3D.

Memorymeyou — Typographic poster Jorrit van Rijt	***Memory — Typographic poster*** Jorrit van Rijt
Typographic poster in a minimalistic style, playing with words, shape and composition.	Starting point was a sentence Jorrit wrote. The sentence 'Even if my memory fades, you won't leave my thoughts', is visually expressed, using a subtle blur to strengten the message.
Occupy Wall Street — Typographic poster Jorrit van Rijt	***From down below — Typographic poster*** Jorrit van Rijt
Typographic poster questioning the meaning of Occupy and the influence of Capitalism.	Playful typographic poster.

Illustrato Typeface　　　　　　　　　　　　　　　　　　　　　　　　　　　　　　　　　Jorrit van Rijt

Illustrato is an illustrative vector typeface in which every single character and number is unique. There are only 'returing' shapes to create cohesion. A time consuming typeface, in which the experiment and the study of combined shapes were the most important ingredients to design the typeface. Sevaral posters show the elegance and aesthetic value of the typeface. The piece of Supremebeing was Jorrit's submission for their typeface competition. It turned out to be the winning entry.

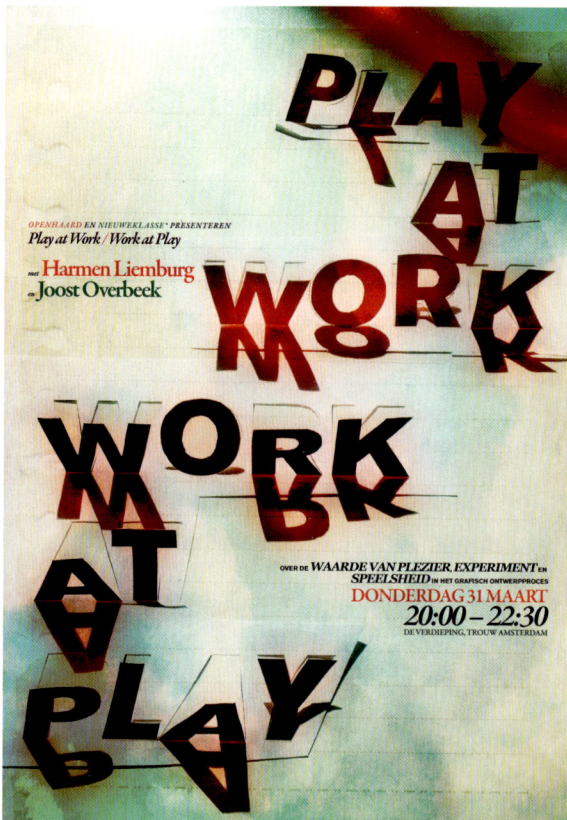

Play at work, Work at play — series of typographic posters Jorrit van Rijt

These posters Jorrit made for a lecture evening, called 'Play at work, Work at play'. He used several techniques, such as stencil and paper cut.

Magnolia & Black Swan — Film posters Jorrit van Rijt

Black Swan: Film poster in which the white swans and the structures of wings create a part of the face of a devilish creature. The black hole leads the viewers attention to the film title, and with a closer look, an eye can be seen. Magnolia: Film poster in which the scene with the frogs falling from the sky, is visually expressed to create a dynamic composition.

Stay hungry, Stay foolish — Jorrit van Rijt

I was inspired by Steve Jobs' speech at the Stanford University in 2005, in which he spoke:"YOU CAN'T CONNECT THE DOTS LOOKING FORWARD; YOU CAN ONLY CONNECT THEM LOOKING BACKWARDS. SO YOU HAVE TO TRUST THAT THE DOTS WILL SOMEHOW CONNECT IN YOUR FUTURE."The work is about complexity and 'connecting the dots'. Each of the lines end with a dot, and every crossing of lines is also connected with a dot. The lines have a connecting, but also a separating function.

ABCDEFGHI
NOPQRSTUVW

abcdefghij
nopqrstuvw

12345678

Loopo Typeface & poster Max Little Design Agency: Little Fonts

Loopo is an experimental typeface based on rotating forms. Characters are created by manipulating each rotation which gives the font a round and fluid look. The modular construction of loopo means that the text creates reference to motion in a playful and eye catching manner. The playful nature of Loopo makes it a great font for posters and other eye catching work including editorial pieces or packaging design.

KLM
XYZ

klm
xyz
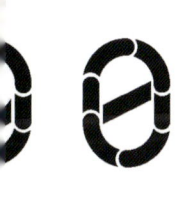

Ministry Of Sound Symbols Campaign — Max Little — Design Agency: Little Fonts

This set of posters was created for a D&AD competition. The symbols on each piece are created by setting the date (09/12, 10/12, 11/12) of each month of events in my own typeface MASS then reflecting them onto each other to create a pattern. The abstract pattern created by setting the dates like this is supposed to conjure visions of other worlds, referencing the escapist nature of going clubbing and leaving the everyday world behind.

226&227

Hyped Font

Medness

Originally designed as a typographic poster for an exhibition titled 'Age of New Generation', this typeface was further developed into a complete typography set titled HYPED font. With its unique characters, it demands to be seen at large!

Nomed Font Medness

Nomed Font is designed based on the simple triangular geometric shape.
Achieve a modern and sophisticated look in your designs by shuffling and stacking the letters into unique compositions.

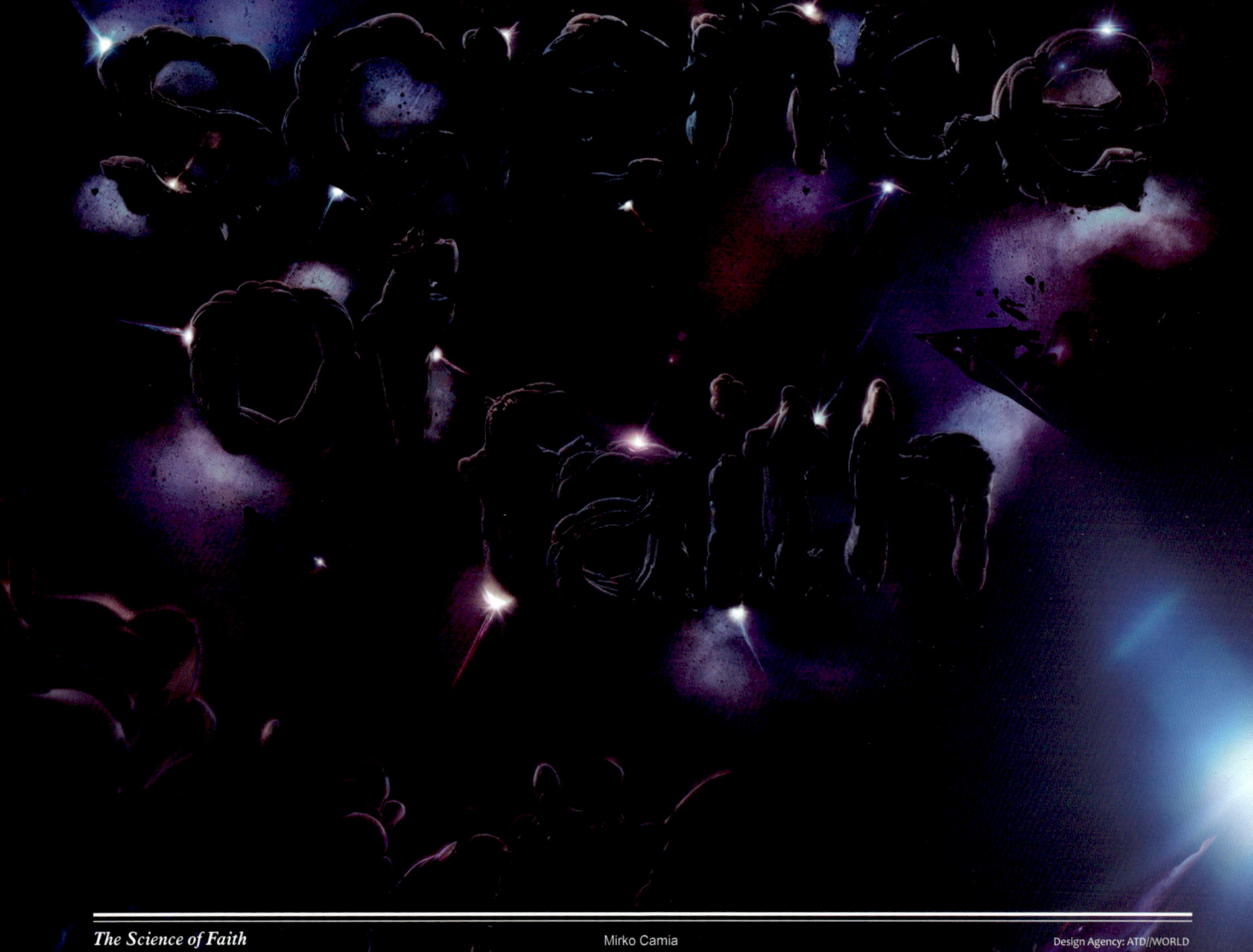

The Science of Faith

Mirko Camia

Design Agency: ATD//WORLD

"THE SCIENCE OF FAITH" illustration has started in July 2011 as an experiment in typography alphabet, based on a font called "magma" will soon available online, but then had a more profound concept.
my idea was to create a great illustration that gave more than one message a sense of the vastness of the sorrounding space.
in the end i used the 3d vision to give it more life.
this is the final risult….

6.829.360.438 PEOPLE ON THIS PLANET MORE THAN 1.000.000.000 PEOPLE SUFFER DUE TO STARVATION THERE HAVE BEEN OVER 30 CONFLICTS WORLDWIDE SINCE '64 RESULTING IN 6.160.950 DEAD

TORTURE VIOLENCE HOMICIDES SUICIDE ATTEMPTS KAMIKAZE STRIKES DEFORESTATION HUNGER THIRST ILLITERACY HUMAN RIGHTS DISEASES NUCLEAR DEVASTATION OIL WATER FOOD UNEMPLOYMENT EXPLOITATION MINES WEAPONRY CONSPIRACY ABDUCTIONS WAR DESPAIR ANGUISH SADNESS RAGE PAIN MADNESS LOSS INSENSIBILITY INCOMPREHENSION DEATH

Numbers & Words

Mirko Camia

Client: You Can Choose Project

The concept was to create a memory plaque, initially developed in 3d but then I decided to create a layout with illustrator, after which I completed the processing 2d with photoshop. I preferred working with a pencil, that using of a program that does it all by himself ..... even though I work 50% with 3D programs, I think that best pieces for an illustrator, leave out directly on the sheet or using a graphics tablet as in my case.
To the letters, I applied a metallic effect, but the most important thing is the lights. The purpose was to light and no light as to mean "that we recognize that of things, if things stand before us."

REMINDER NOT TO FORGET
SAVE YOUR LIFE
SAVE THE WORLD

Hipnosys — Mirko Camia — Design Agency: ATD//WORLD

The concept was to simulate the breakage of a lens of the spectacles, giving a sensation of suction to the word Hipnosys. I built the effect with alternating stripes of color, then adding with photoshop a lot of soft colors to give a sense of blur.
The modeling was done in Cinema 4d, as well as the lights and if you look at the picture carefully you can see under the letters a lot of depth, but is actually an optical illusion. I really enjoyed myself.

Vectory Font — Mirko Camia — Design Agency: ATD//WORLD
Client: Commercial Typeface

VECTORY FONT name derives from three things, V for victory, V for revenge and finally a song by N.E.R.D.
I developed all in vector with illustrator and was also very tiring because it was my first typeface designed entirely with the tablet.
I wanted a font a bit long and very sci-fi but that could also be used for trade.

YOU CAN CHOOSE # 2   Mirko Camia   Design Agency: ATD//WORLD

"YOU CAN CHOOSE #2" is an illustration which is part of a publishing project YYC.
Develops almost completely in vector-style, has been given a sense of freshness both in style, both as brightly colors.

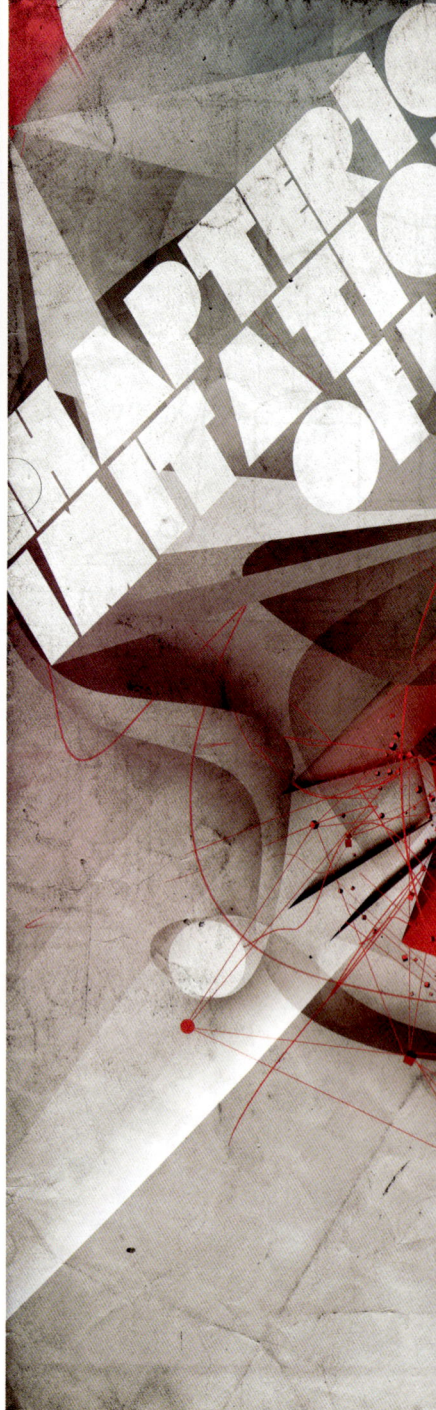

Kaboom, Suit Up, 2012 Chapter 10, Water Vladimir Tomin

Kaboom was promotional work for my free hand-made plasticine font. Suit Up was part of exhibition at slashthree.com and features Barny Stinson, character of "How I Met Your Mother" TV series. 2012 Chapter 10 was illustration for a online book project called "Twenty Twelve". This was cover for 10th chapter. Water was personal project "inspired" by fire occurred in house we live.

Quote Unquote Vladimir Tomin

Opening sequence for www.slashthree.com artpack called "Quote Unquote".

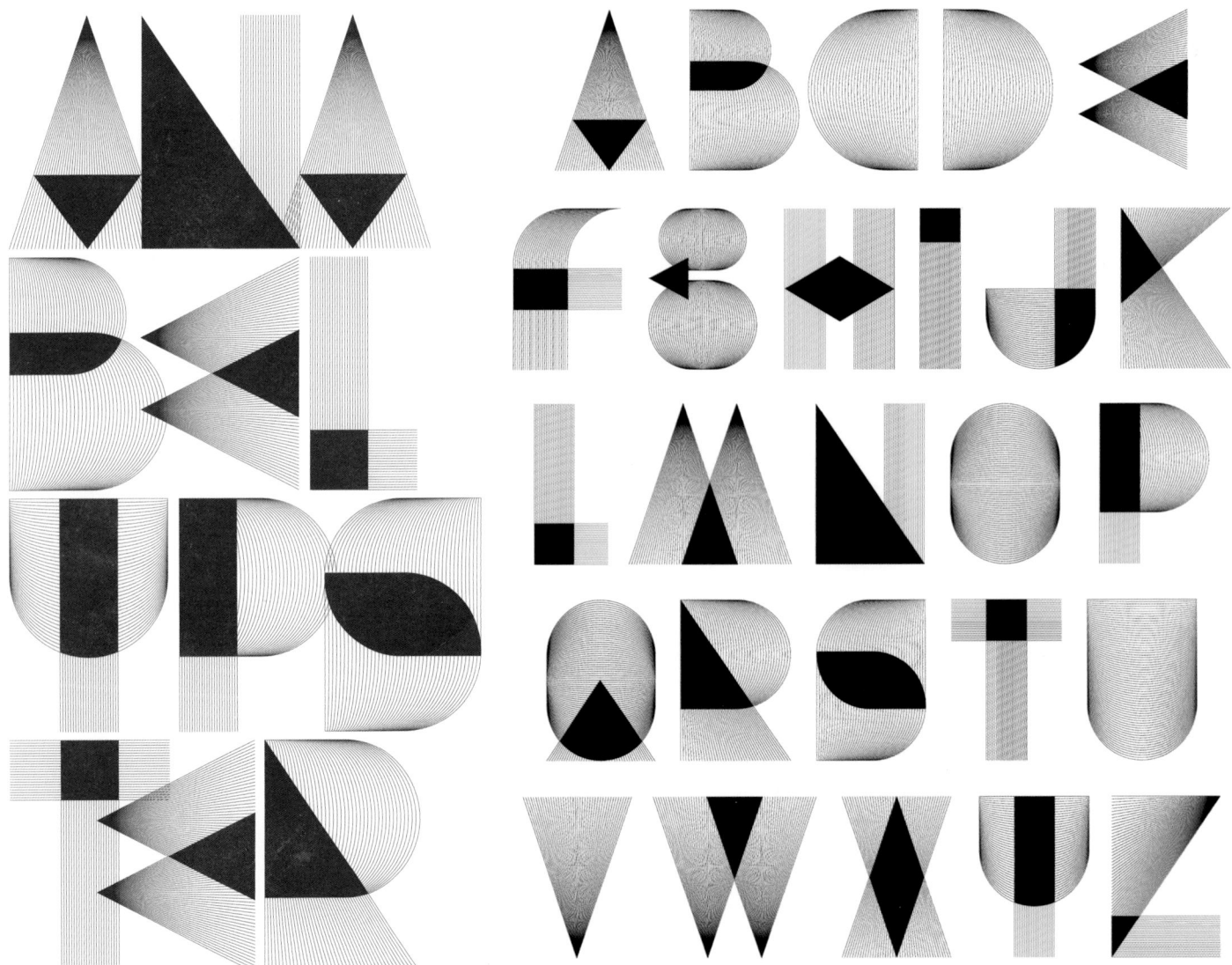

Anabelypster Font Patrick Seymour

I like optical illusions, see people around me look at my work and say: I like it but my eyes hurt. I think I managed to create this effect with my font Anabelypster.

ABCDE
FGHIJK
LMNOP
QRSTU
VWXYZ

merry Xmas

joyeux noël

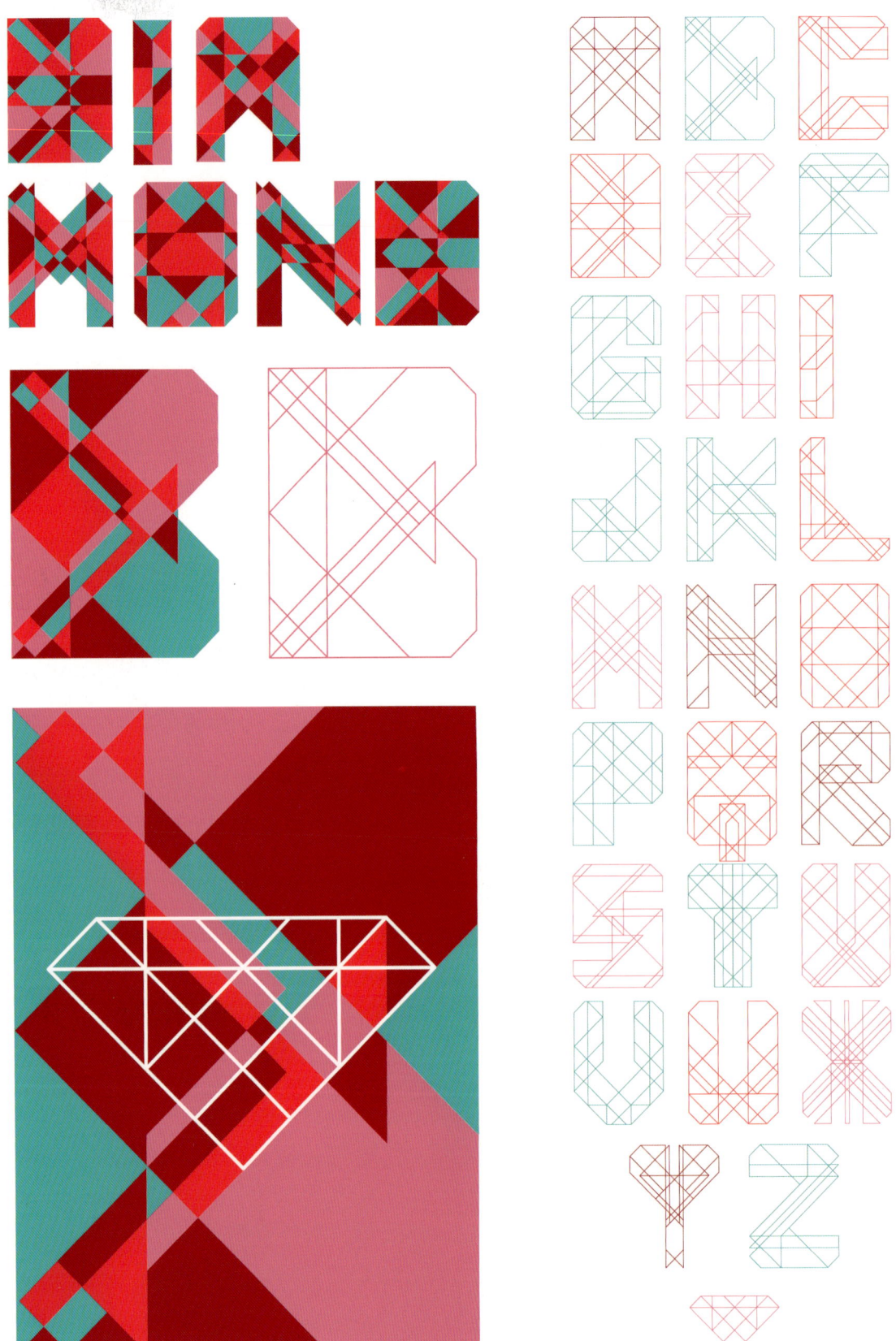

Diamond Font　　　　　　　　　　　　　　　　　　　Patrick Seymour

My "Diamond" font had basically 2 basic visual rules, I drew lines and my limitation as for what to do with the lines is that those had to be drwn straight or at a 45 degree angle, that created dozens of little "cells" wich once filled with color gave the strange impression that the surface was mirrored like a diamond.

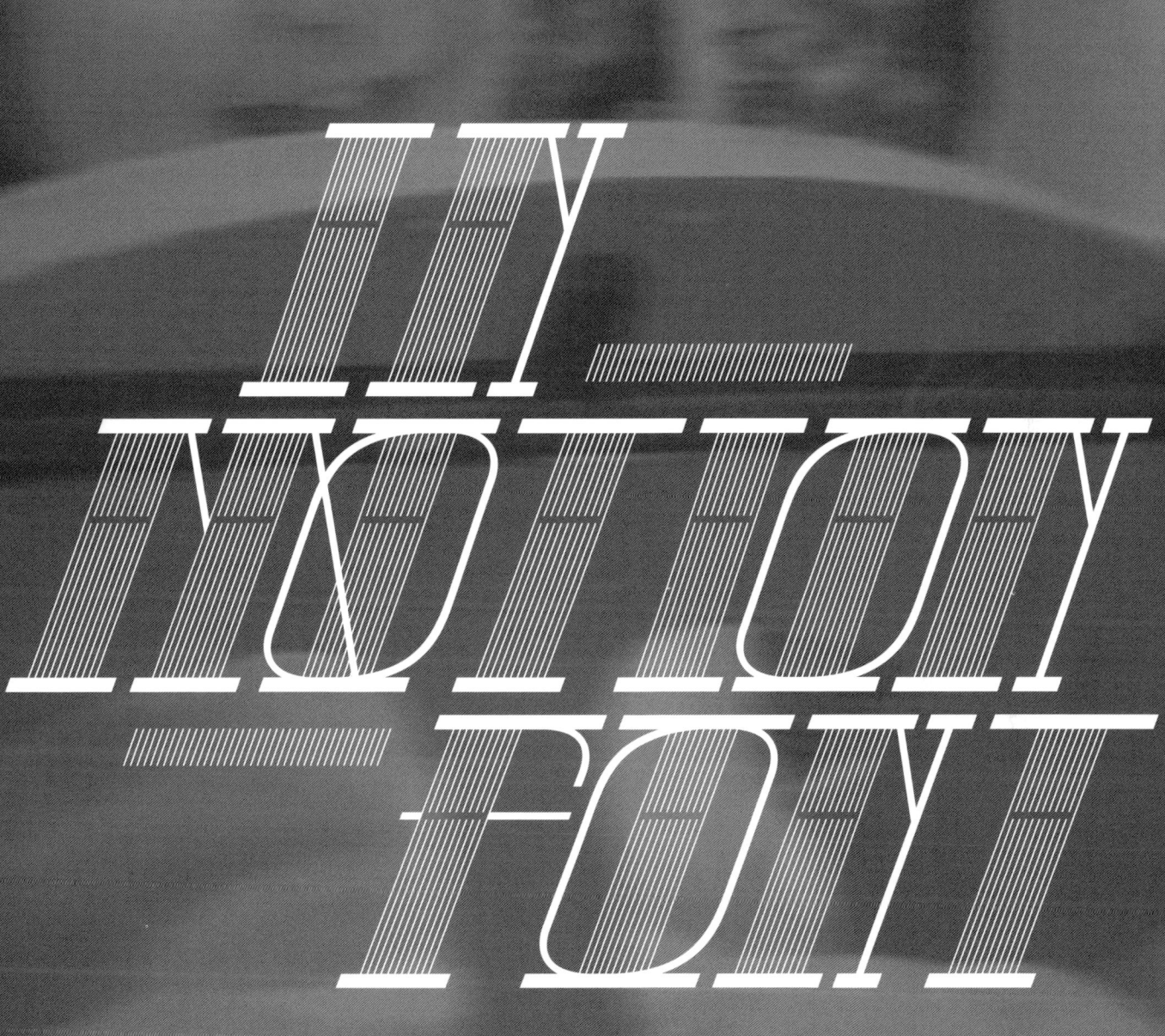

In Motion Font

Patrick Seymour

In this typography, the effect is created by the succession of eleven diagonal lines. When the letters are in close-up, it is clear that these are stable and solid lines, but once you zoom out, they appear to be in motion.

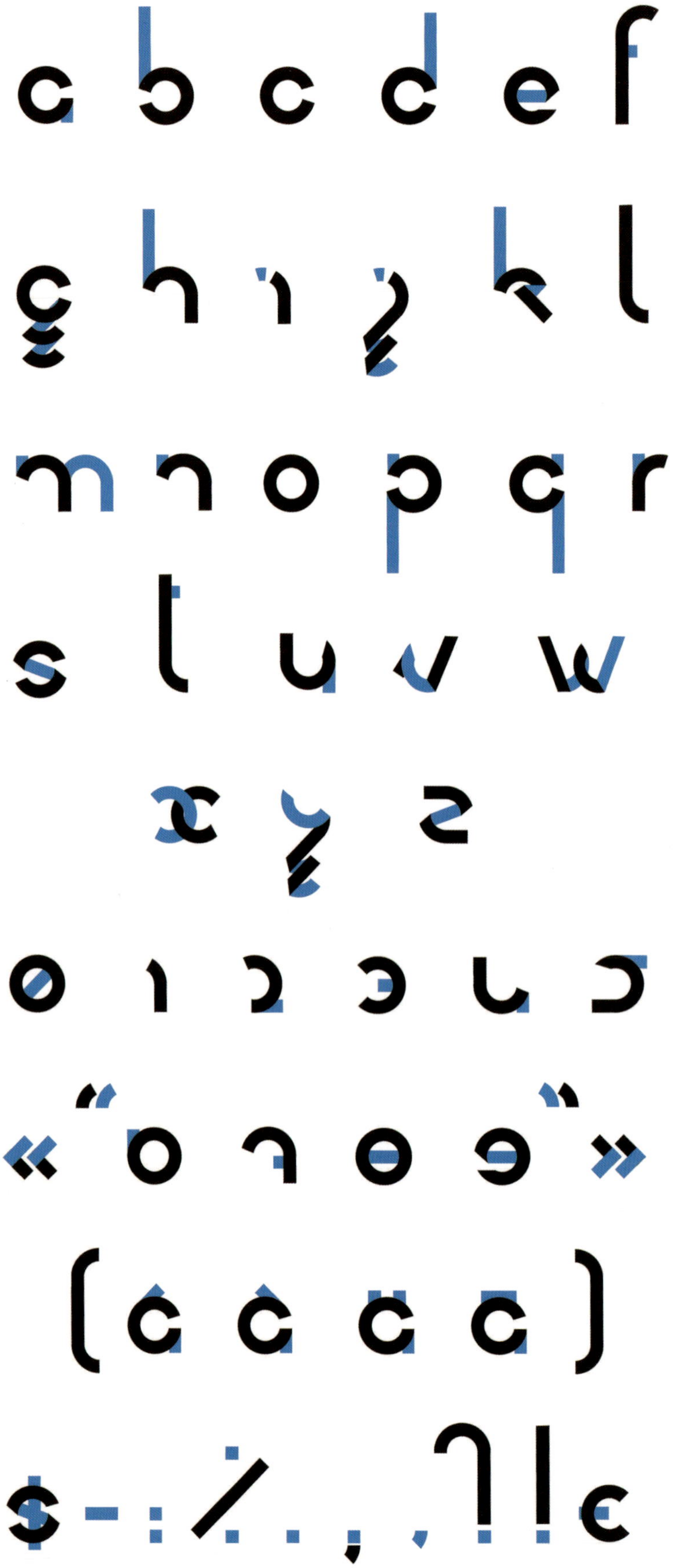

Fold Type

Philippe Nicolas

Modern decorative font

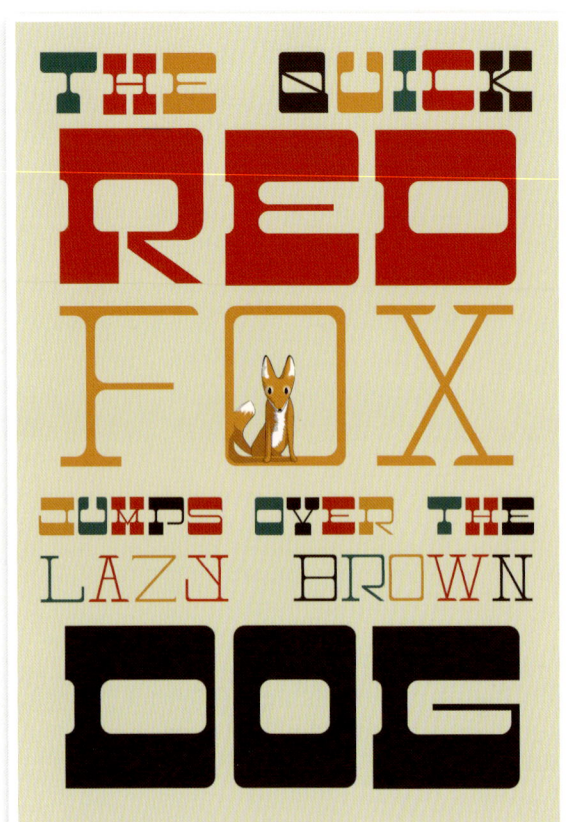

Bang-Bang — Philippe Nicolas

Slab Serif typeface family, 5 styles

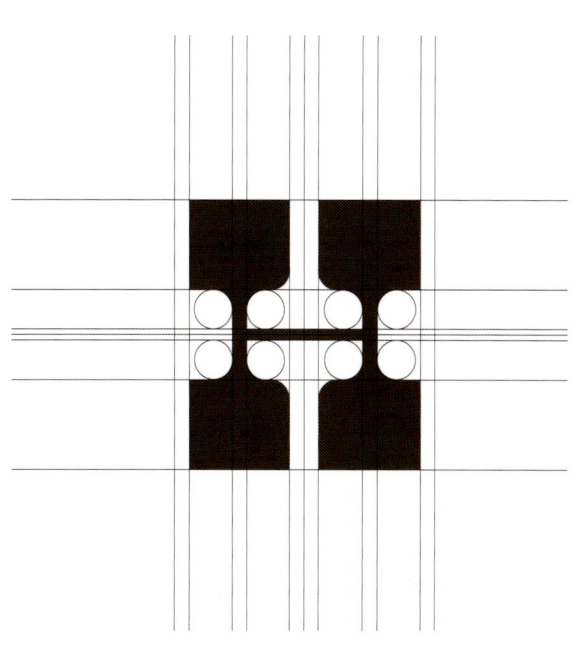

2012 Photonica

This is my only work with numbers.

Music Photonica

Well, this poster is very simple, I always listen to music when I am designing, so it is the best combination!

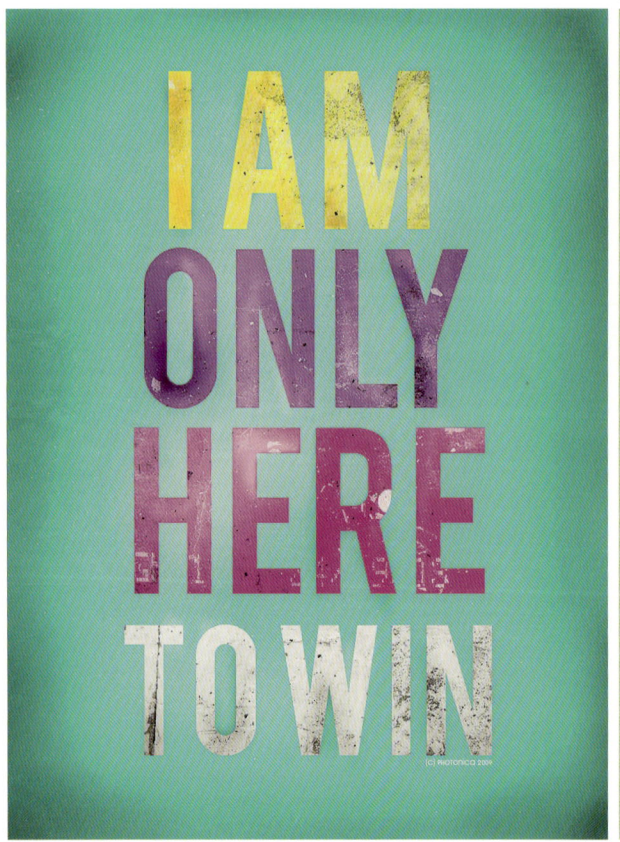

Can you feel it coming?   Photonica

I usually inspire myself in songs, this typography is an example of that, it is inspired in a song from a British band called Kasabian. I hope you listen the song, you will like it.

No olvido los sueños   Photonica

this is my only typography with a Spanish phrase, It means 'I never forget my dreams' We must not forget our own dreams, dream is free, and it one of the most important thing that we have.

I am only here to win   Photonica

This is the first typography that I designed, so it is very important for me.

I am too afraid to love you   Photonica

It's other of my works where I mix typographies and shapes, I really like de colors. This design is also inspire in a song, from the band The Black Keys.

Love Typography

Photonica

I think this one is my favorite typography, I love the mix of the shapes with the different kind of typographies, and of course the color palette. Typography is my favorite part of graphic design, yes, I admit that I am totally in love with typography art.

I want to touch the other side   Photonica

My last typography, inspired in one of my favorite songs, Map of th Problematique, by MUSE.

Last night a DJ *save my life* Photonica

This line belongs to a famous songs, I usually don't work with 3D shapes, this poster is only an execption.

AMP Capital - Volatility   Toby And Pete   Design Agency: Banjo Advertising

AMP Capital is a capital investment branch of AMP. Once again we were engaged to personify market volatility and a sense of risk management.

AMP - Growth — Toby And Pete — Design Agency: Banjo Advertising

Growth and Secure are part of an ongoing collaboration between Banjo Advertising and Toby and Pete for their client AMP.

AMP - Secure Toby And Pete Design Agency: Banjo Advertising

Growth and Secure are part of an ongoing collaboration between Banjo Advertising and Toby and Pete for their client AMP.
As part of AMP's branding we created personifications of some of the core values of AMP, a wealth management company active in Australia and New Zealand.

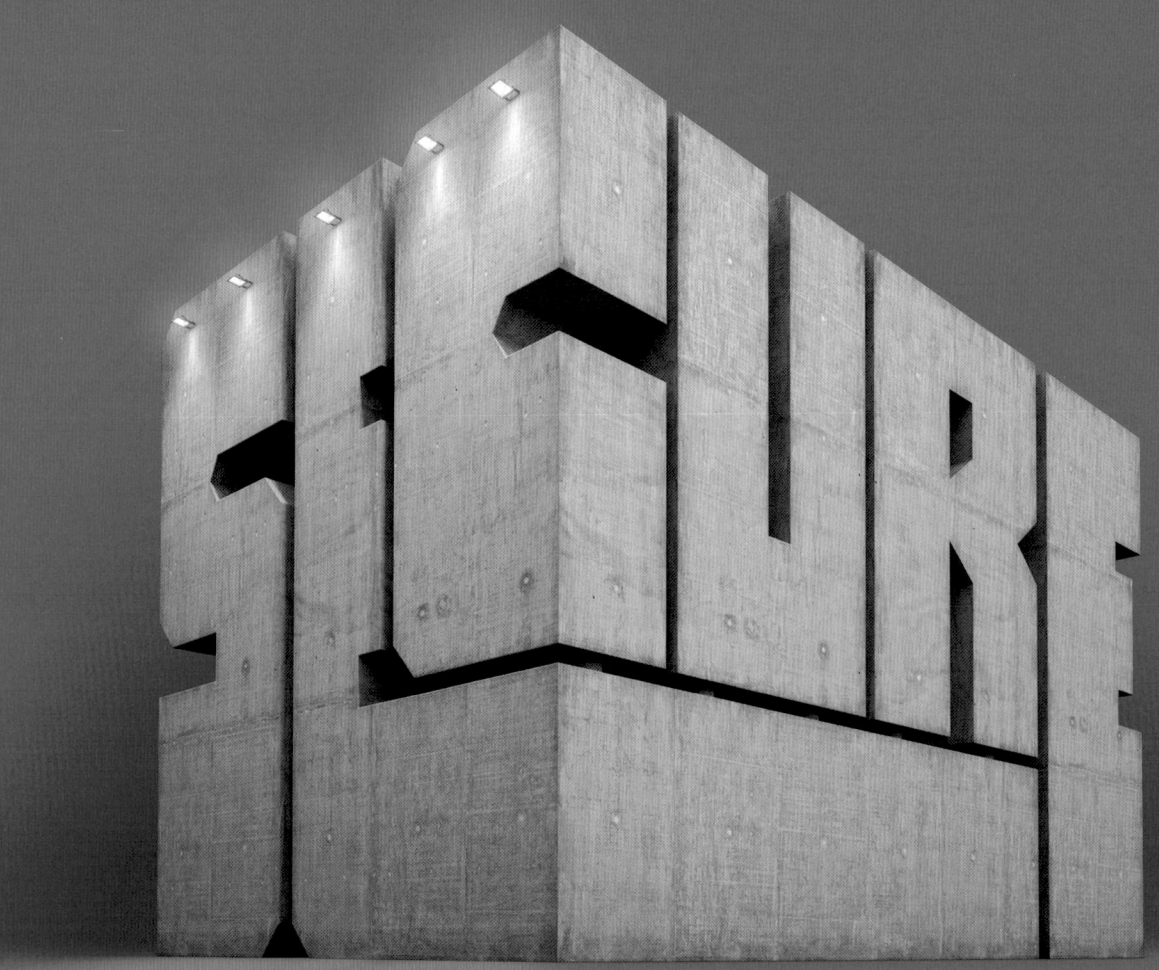

Kellogg's All Bran — Toby And Pete — Client: JWT Sydney

We were charged with designing some type to illustrate the bloated feeling some experience and at the same time subsequent relief offered by sufficient dietary fibre intake.

Steve Back Toby And Pete

The creative director Steve Back approached us with a brief to promote his personal folio.
The brief was simply "make it fun, make it a jumping castle, make me want to go there"

Toby And Pete Name Cards   Toby And Pete

A self promotional project to illustrate that Toby And Pete is no longer just Toby And Pete but an umbrella name for a collective of artists.

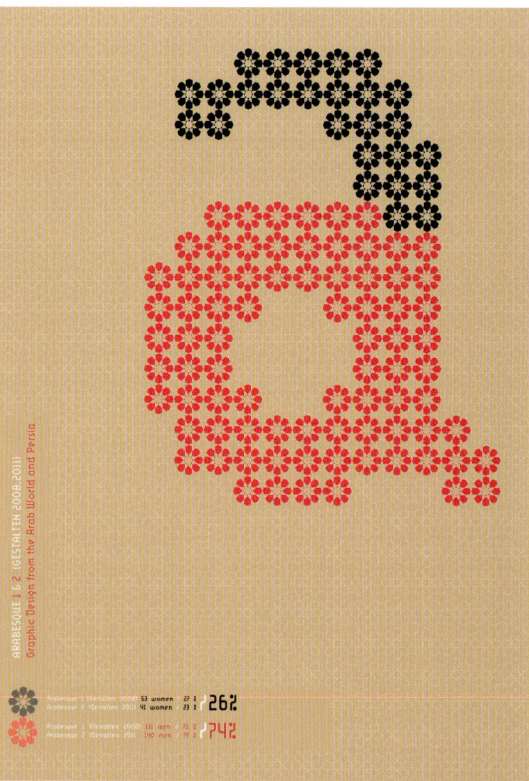
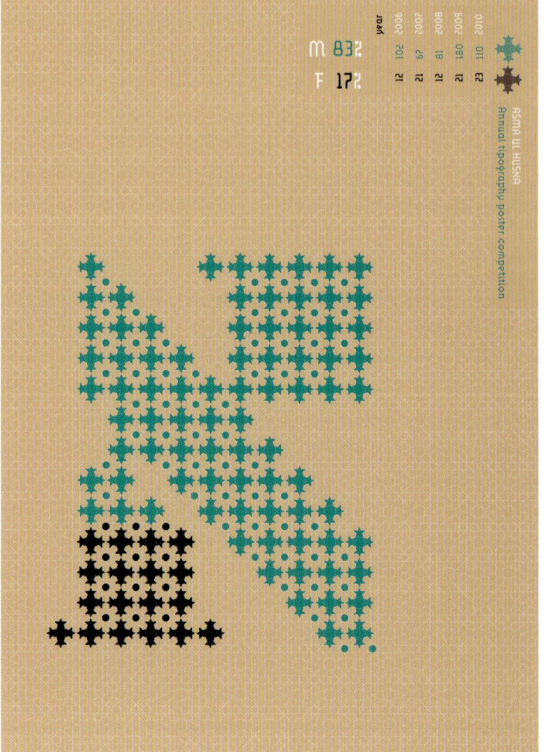

Women in graphic design- Arabesque Ágnes Jekli Client: MOME- university project

Infographics about the women's place in arabian and iranian graphic design. The first poster with the red A is based on information of a european collection of contemporary arabian graphic design collected from two books of Gestalten- Arabesque 1, Gestalten 2008, and Arabesque 2, Gestalten 2011 . The blue "alef" is based on a research on the participants of Asma Ul Husna- an annual iranian typographic poster competition. The two signs together shows the complete result of the research

Optypo — Ágnes Jekli — Client: MOME- university project

Optypo typeface was created for OPTYPO exhibition in 2010, which was about the renessaince of Opart in contemporary graphic design. Optypo is a display typeface which uses just basic geometric shapes, and it was used for the typographic poster as well.

AGIKO *project* Ágnes Jekli, Anikó Kőhegyes Client: MOME- university project

The aim of the synthesis project was to find the connections between different creative attitudes and to search for a common conclusion. The AGIKO project is reflecting on the common "ars poetica" of the creators. The name "AGIKO' is a mosaic word created by using the letters of the names of the group members. The alphabet created specially for the project contains several elements, and the constellation of these elements is giving the possibility to create new letters and forms, new combinations. The aim of the RELAX project is to create skill developing games which have relaxing effect at the same time.
The AGIKO cube: the names of the creators- ANIKO and AGI- contain 6 letters. This number was the base of choosing the cube as form to use its 6 sides. By turning the sides of the cube the different element are giving the possibility to create new letters and forms, to make new combinations.
The AGIKO puzzle contains 108 elements, which allows to create any letter or form easily.

Take it easy.
Kőhegyes Anikó & Jekli Ágnes

Letters Ágnes Jekli Client: MOME- university project

This project uses the two translations of the hungarian word: LEVELEK, because it means LETTERS and LEAVES at the same time. This ambiguity gave me the possibility, to express LEVELEK on two ways.

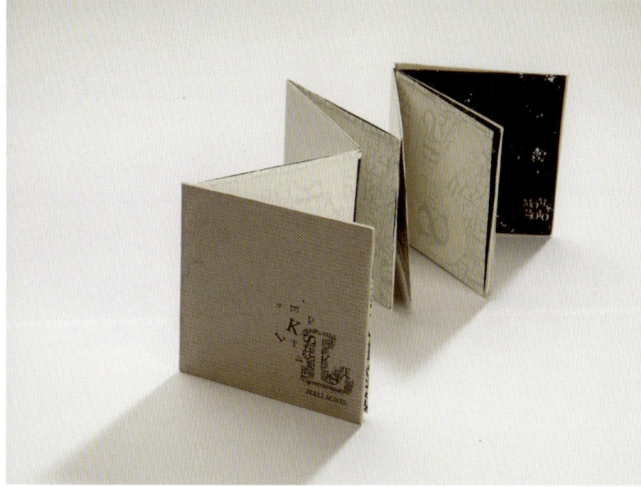

Virtuous Bao Nguyen

Personal typographic design

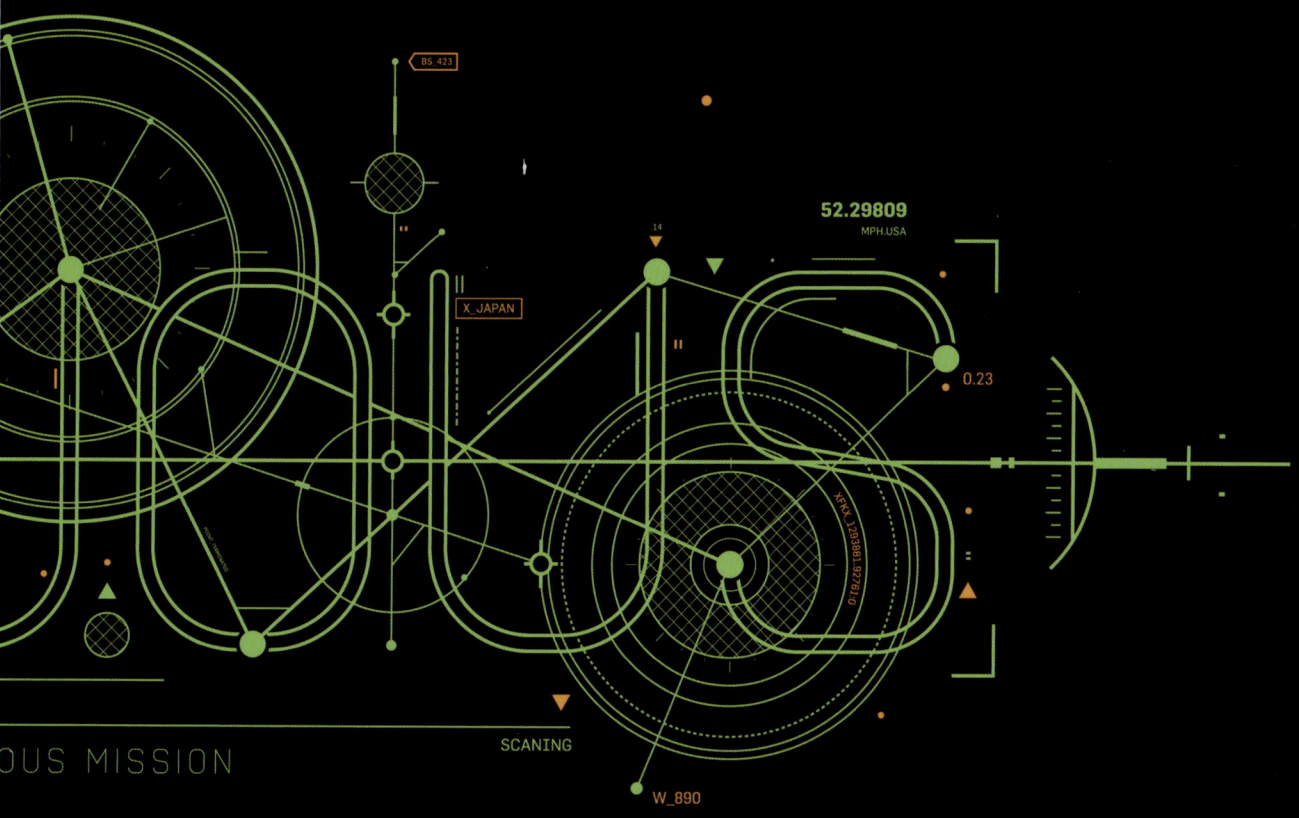

I feel good today — Niels Buschke — Design Agency: SANTIAGO DESIGN — Client: Two Wheels Good — Photographer: Santiago Design

This temporary wall art was created by designer and artist Niels Buschke (SANTIAGO DESIGN) to promote urban mobility. Buschke was asked by the bike shop Two Wheels Good to create something unique that would draw the attention of an audience wether they are affine for cycling or not. The chosen location for this temporary installation was the well known „erste liebe bar" (German for „first love") in the citycenter of Hamburg.
Buschke decided to create a three-dimensional wall art. As a focal point he used a Viktor bike by German manufacturer Schindelhauer. The white bike strikes through its pure design and futuristic carbon drive. Starting from this extraordinary bike he arranged various imaginative illustrations, modern typography in combination with intelligent writing that works as a statement. Viewed from a certain distance the Viktor bike becomes part of the writing „I feel good today".

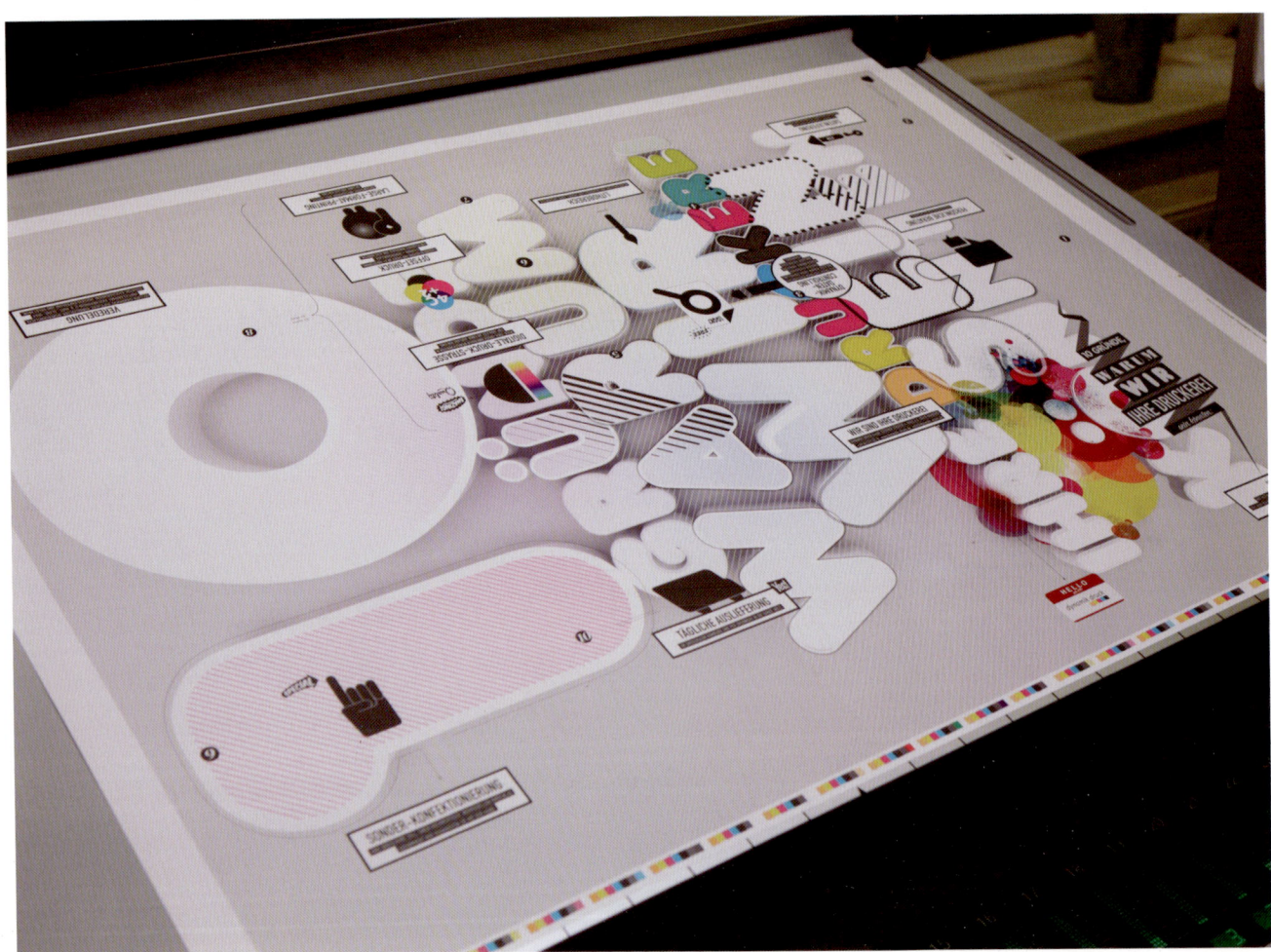

Zehn Gründe warum wir Ihre Druckerei sein könnten Niels Buschke

Design Agency: SANTIAGO DESIGN
Client: Dynamik Druck (Dynamic Print)

Dynamik Druck is an Offset-Printinting Company. A handcrafted presentation box, within a plexiglass tube filled with shredded printing company names (competitors) is the heart of the promotion tools. An accompanying poster is illustrating ten reasons, why to print at Dynamik Druck (Dynamic Print).

TÄGLICHE AUSLIEFERUNG Yes!
IM GROSSRAUM HAMBURG UND PER OVERNIGHT IN DIE GANZE WELT.

WIR SIND IHRE DRUCKEREI
DYNAMIK DRUCK GmbH · ESSENER STRASSE 4, HAUS 6 A, 22419 HAMBURG
+49 40 537137−0 · www.dynamik-druck.de · info@dynamik-druck.de

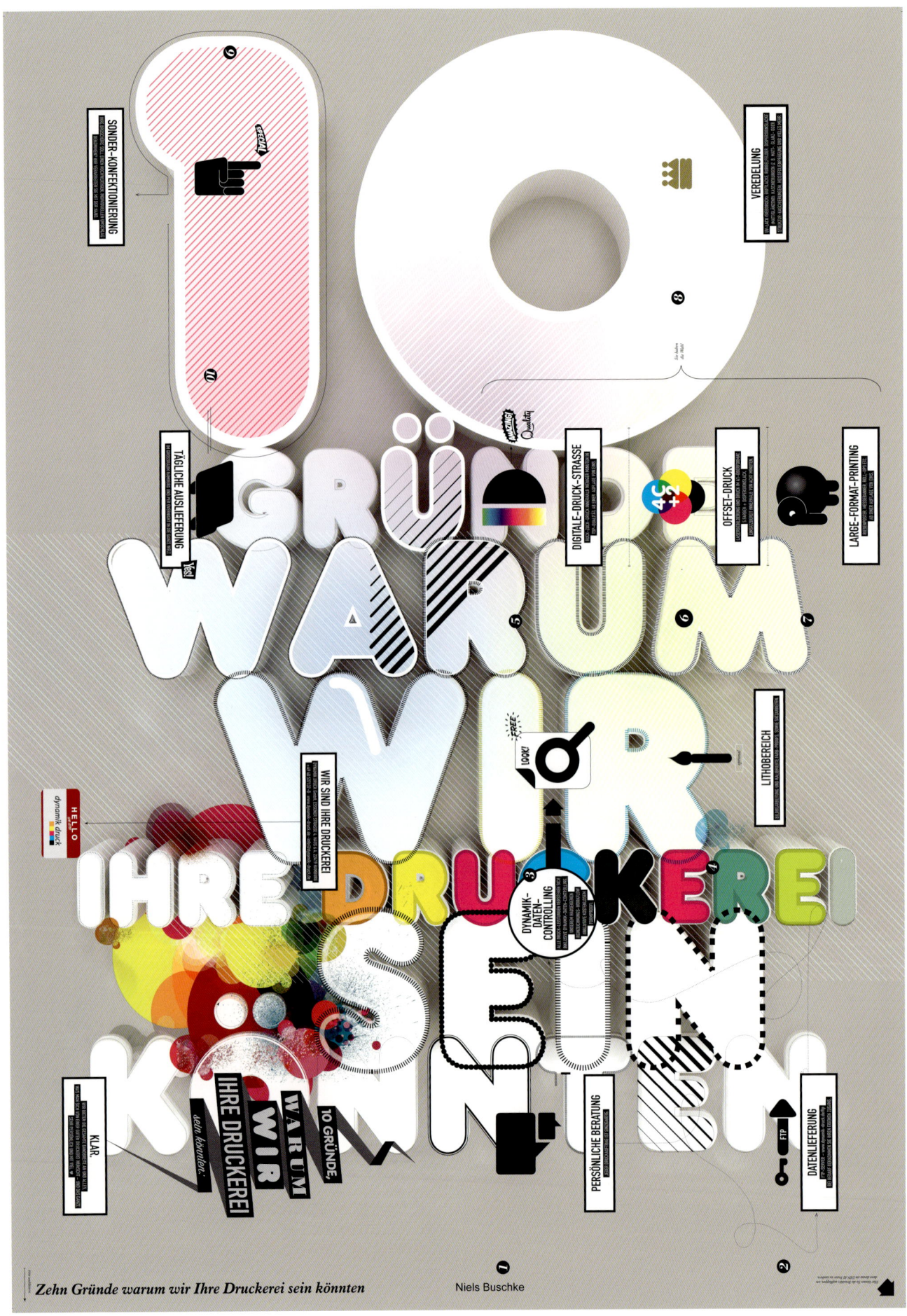

274&275

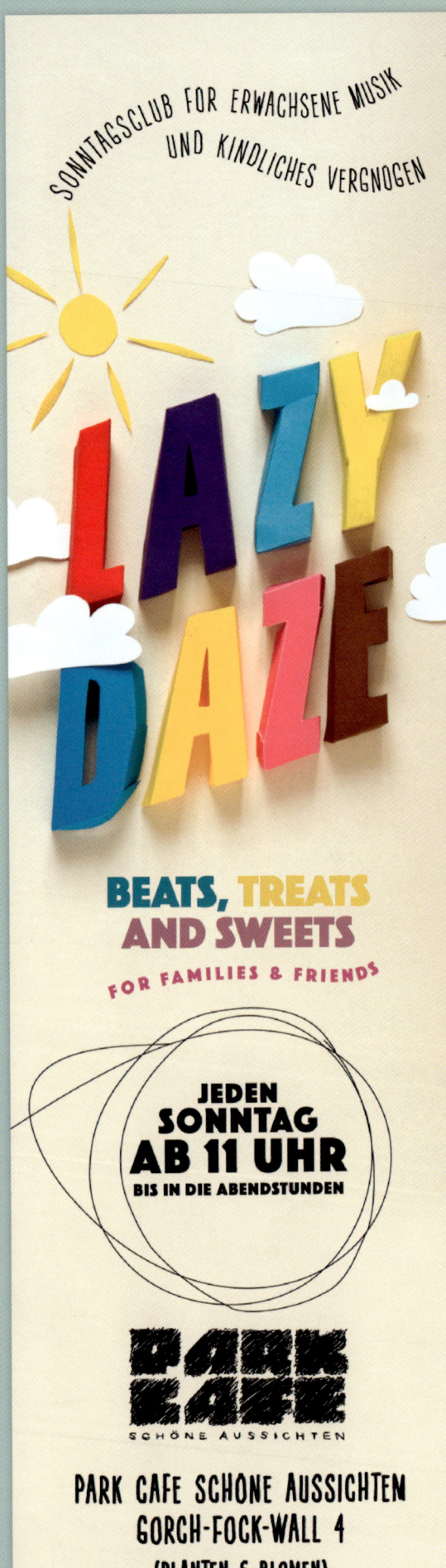
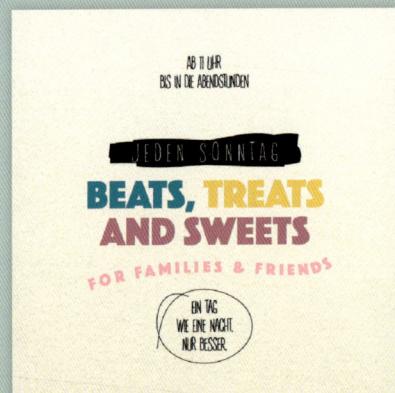

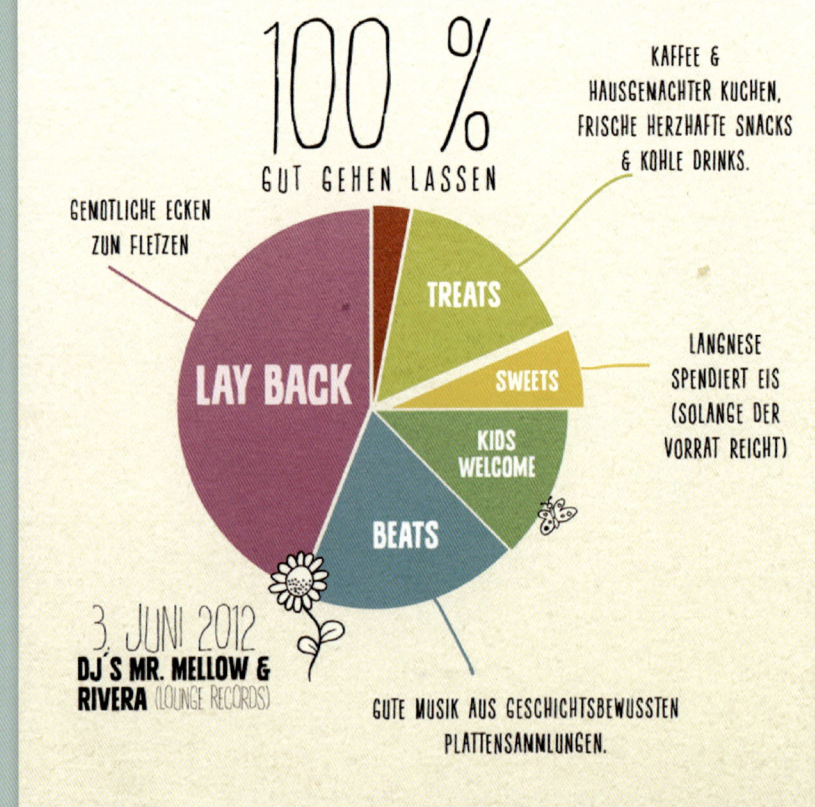

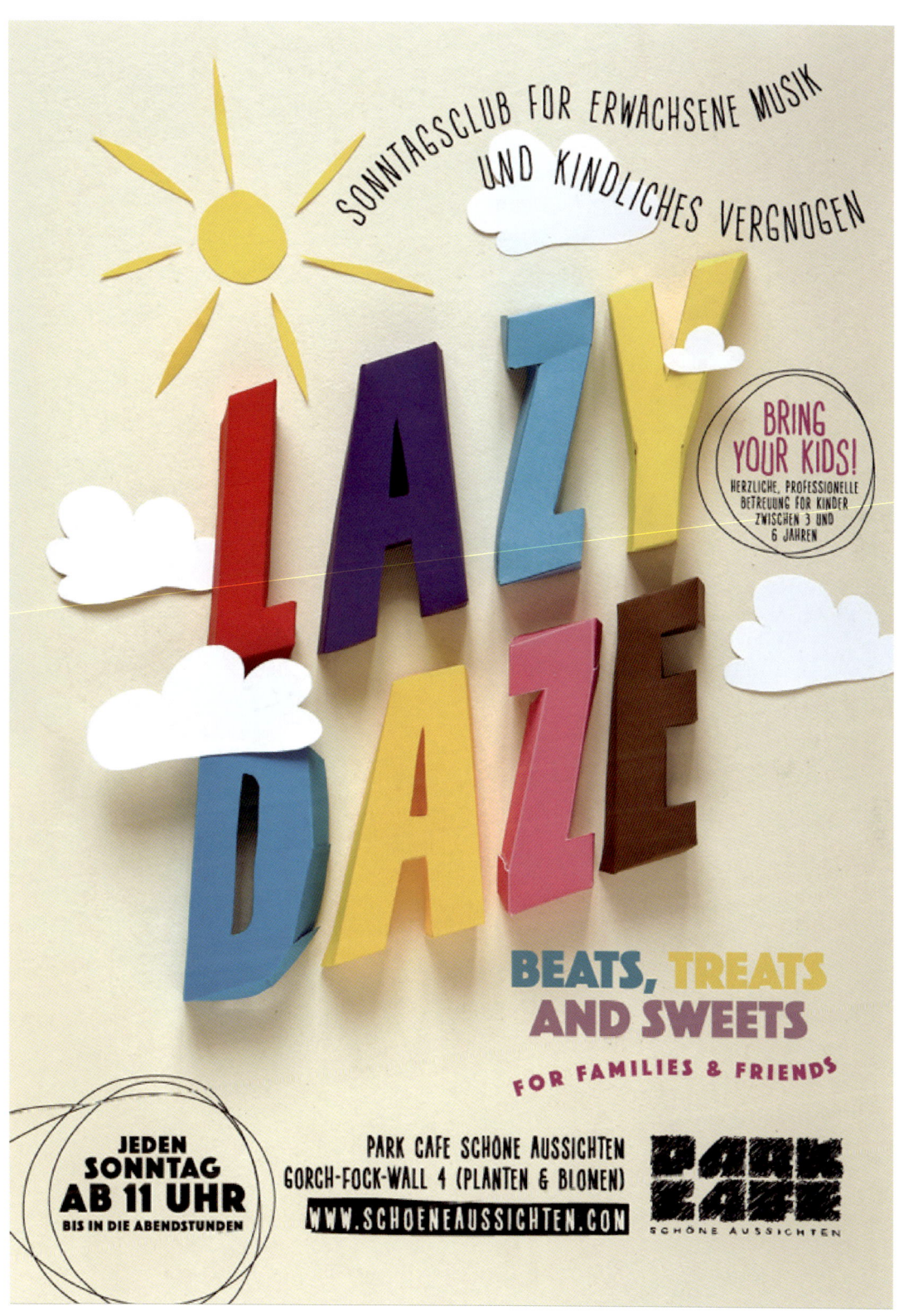

LAZY DAZE

Niels Buschke

Design Agency: SANTIAGO DESIGN
Client: Park Cafe

LAZY DAZE (Lazy Days) is an event-series on sundays with focused on family and child entertainment. The promotional designs are based on a simple-hearted style to mirror idleness and childhood.

Let's make great things — Niels Buschke — Design Agency: SANTIAGO DESIGN

A handcrafted silksreen Edition (6 prints in red/6 prints in blue) with a machine drawn outline.

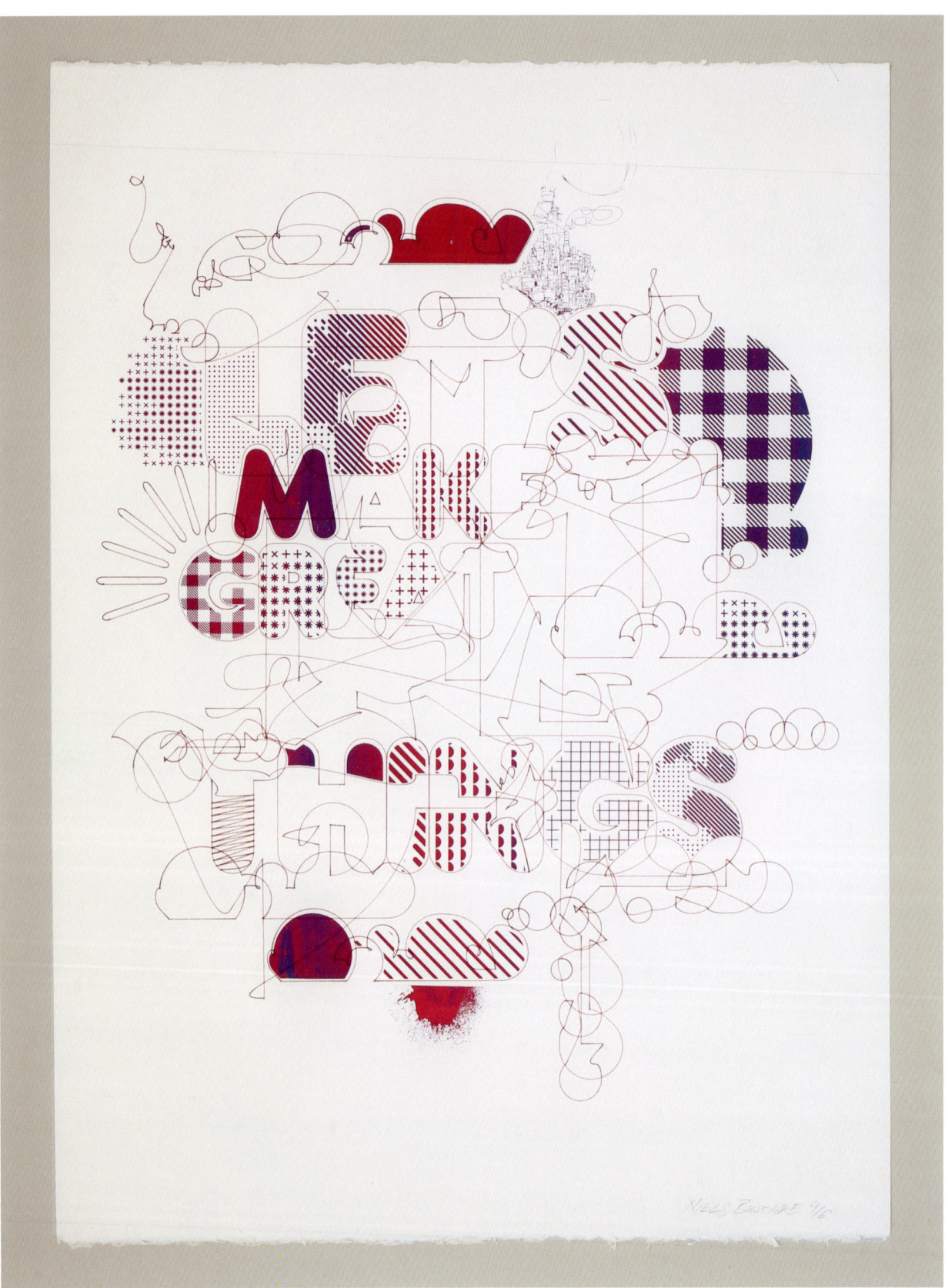

Let's make great things

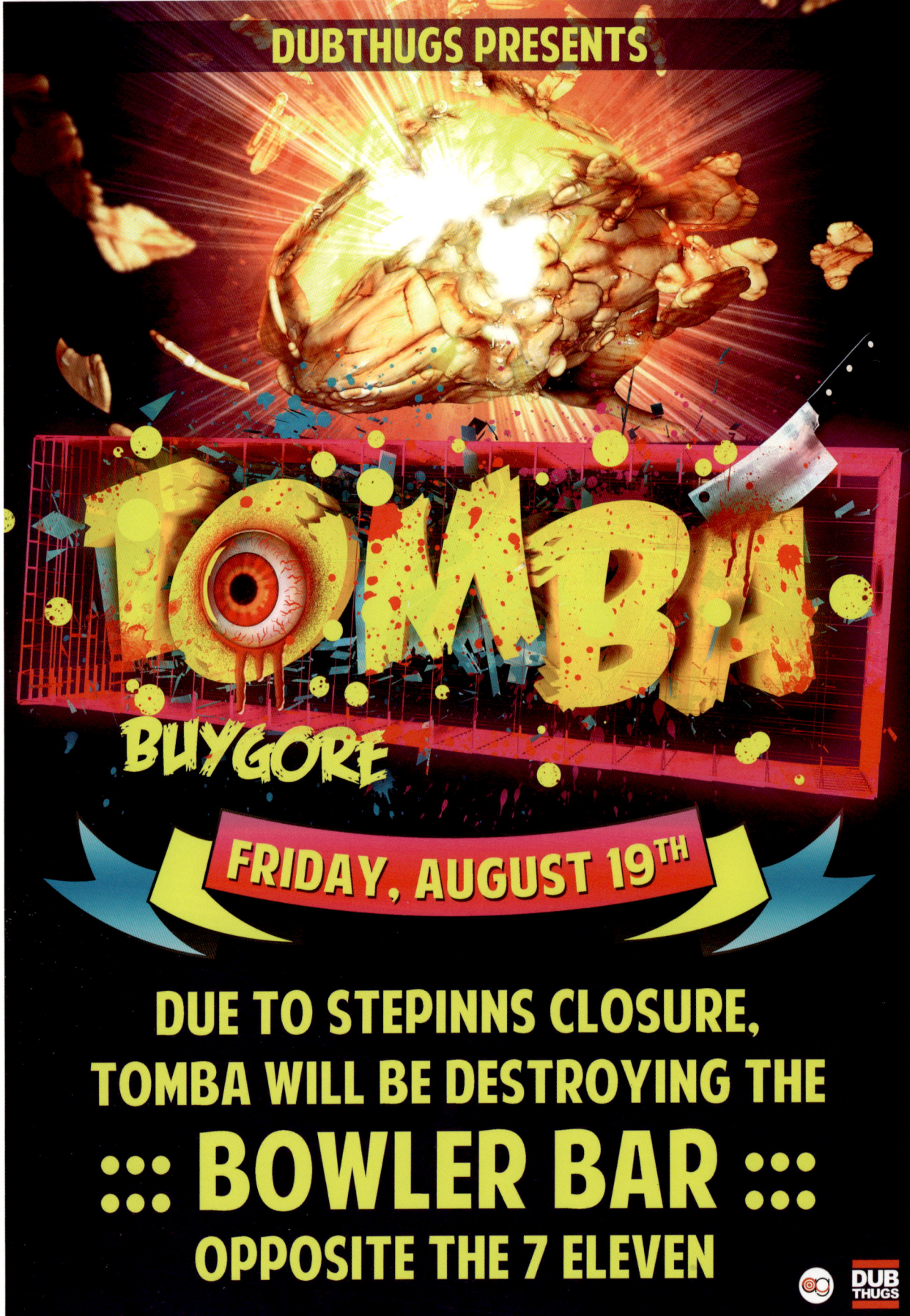

Tomba Poster

Anthony Gargasz

Client: Dub Thugs Brisbane (AUS)

Commissioned Work

KOAN Sound NYE Poster — Anthony Gargasz — Client: Dub Thugs Brisbane(AUS) — *Helicopter Showdown Poster*

Commissioned Work — Commissioned Work

Funtcase, Gemini, & Inspector Dubplate Poster

Commissioned Work

Borgore Fan Art Anthony Gargasz

Personal work, def will bring it to his attention to!

World Domination — Anthony Gargasz — Client: Dub Thugs Brisbane (AUS)

Commissioned Work

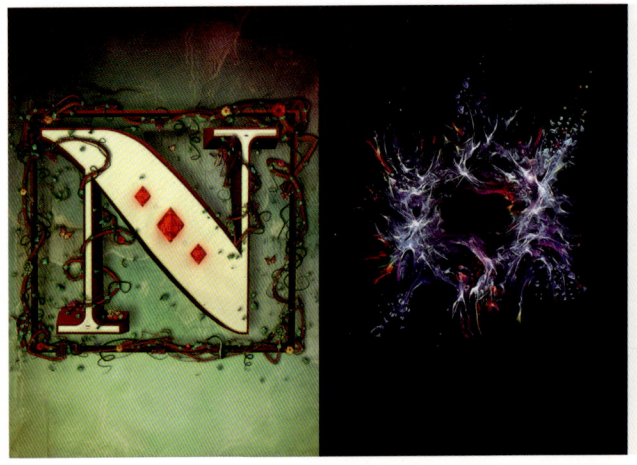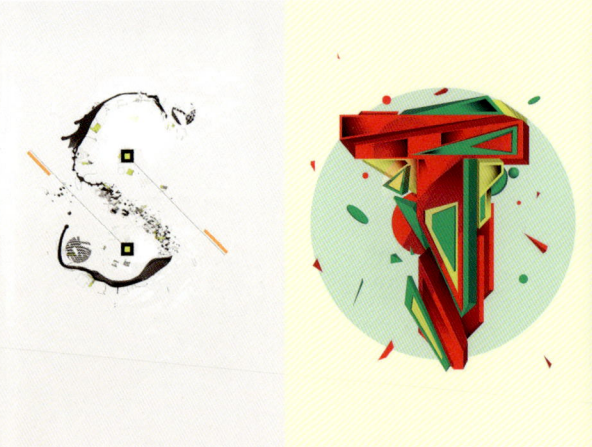

Intrinsic Nature — Anthony Gargasz

Digital artwork created for digital media collective Intrinsic Nature

Nostalgia   Anthony Gargasz

After valiant effort, we proudly present the first exhibition of 2012. Our 27th release, Nostalgia, brings a dynamic collection of art, photography, and music. The term "Nostalgia" was interpreted in a unique manner amongst our international roster. Feelings of sorrow, felicity, and childhood memories were ignited within and translated into ethereal works of art. We even journeyed back into EvokeOne's past by creating our "Nostalgia" type group collaboration that was directed by Brandon Spahn. This was an idea we presented three years ago in our "Revolution" release, and enjoyed revisiting this type project to bring our artists together.

Joaquin Palting Photography Anthony Neil Dart Design Agency - Ontwerp.TV
Client: JP Photography

Experimental graphic series for self-promotional purposes – non-profit work. I was approached by Joaquin Palting to collaborate on a photographic project for promotional purposes.

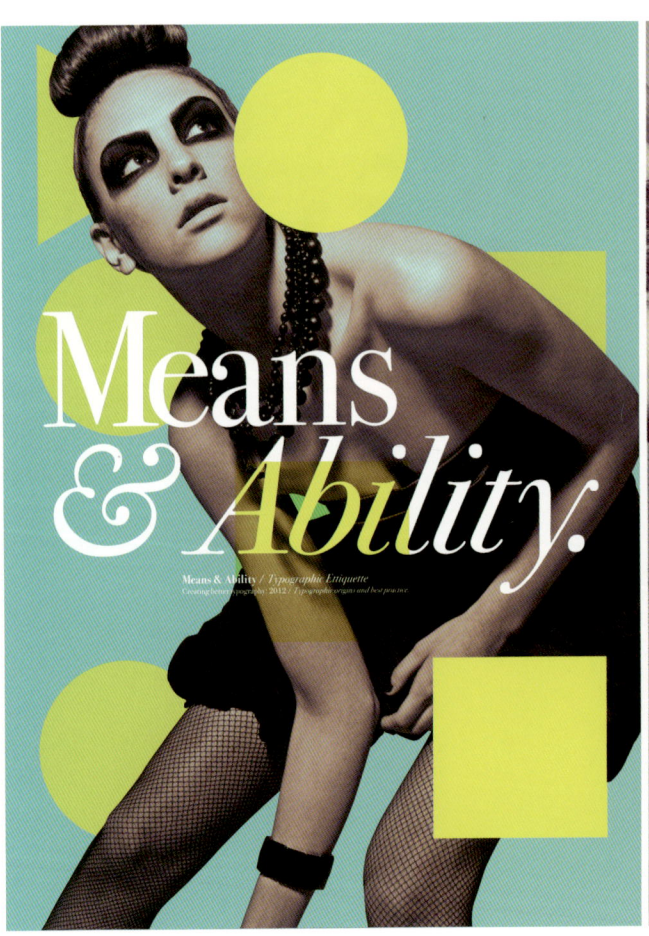

Typographic Moodsetter

Anthony Neil Dart

Design Agency: Ontwerp.tv
Client: AND
Photographer: Royalty free stock images

Experimental graphic series for self-promotional purposes – non-profit work. This series
Continues a ongoing fascination for the exploration of type versus image.

Work In Progress   Anthony Neil Dart   Design Agency: Ontwerp.tv
Client: AND
Photographer: Royalty free stock images

Experimental graphic series for self-promotional purposes – non-profit work. This series
Continues a ongoing fascination for the exploration of type versus image.

FILTER017 APPAREL Filter017 Designer: Enzo Lin, Wen Ko
Client: Filter017 CREALIVE Photographer: Enzo Lin

The RGB style of cross stitching exploration of color combination creates some dramatic effects. The print effect can never be achieved in stitch and it's interesting to see as typeface. RGB Stitch Alphabet is a typographic experiment, a set of 26 sans-serif uppercase letter forms. Each letter is handmade using a combination of two overlapping RGB colors. The colors are lines of 90 and 45 degrees handmade cross-stitch. The idea of RGB Alphabet grew out of my interest in handmade typography, the connections between color and form.

FILTER017 CARVED SKATEBOARD "SCREAMING PARTY"-TRIBUTE TO JIM PHILLIPS

Filter017

Designer: Enzo Lin, Wen Ko
Client: SANTA CRUZ & PARADISE   Photographer: Enzo Lin

Filter017 participate in skateboard artist Jim Phillip-The Dreamers exhibition at the end of 2011.
We used to good layout and humorous graphics re-interpretation of the classic graphics of Jim Phillip.

FILTER017 LEATHER WALLET & COIN CASE　　　　Filter017

Designer: Enzo Lin, Wen Ko
Client: Filter017 CREALIVE
Photographer: Enzo Lin

Filter017 commissioned has many years experience in production of leather goods manufacturers.
In addition to using the material in the wallet real leather making, sewing and workmanship is also very delicate.
Showed a large area Filter017 PATTERN 3D embossed, constantly trying to develop.
Finally launched in 2011, the classic Razzle Dazzle series of leather goods.

FILTER017 X URBAN GRAPHIC WRAPPERING PAPER SERIES

Filter017

Designer: Enzo Lin, Wen Ko
Client: URBAN GRAPHIC
Photographer: Enzo Lin

Filter017 is honored to be from the British contemporary art and design units Urban Graphic invited to authorize the joint production of five Filter017 wrapping papers.

Dulux Colour Awards Josip Kelava Creative Director: Damian Royce
Art Director: Quenton Miller   Client: Dulux

A direct mail kit that announces the Dulux Colour Awards Competition has commenced. A collection of posters showing the famous colours of history created in a stylized infographic, advertises you add your own colours to history.

Geomas Josip Kelava

Ever listened to a piece of music and got inspired? Well this was the case for the creation of Geomas. It was inspired by the sounds of dubstep, with it's premeditated and structured sounds. From these sounds, I wanted to create something that felt futuristic, bold, calculated and systematic. And thus, Geomas was born. It's funny how music can do that to you.

Coco Vodka — Josip Kelava — Client: Coco Vodka

Coco Vodka is a very smooth and clean spirit which made in the high lands of Netherlands. It is made using the pure waters from the Vaalserberg and is distilled six times from "non-genetically modified" European wheat. With a rich Dutch background, I used the infamous colour of orange to motivate my design and reference the mountain ranges of the Netherlands.

THE URBAN FASHION DREAM

Mass production means that more clothes are now available at lower costs, which means cutting corners on production and labour while contributing to environmental damage through dyes and excess material waste. Georgia McCorkill's Red Carpet Project encourages eco-friendly fashion on the catwalk, whereby high-profile names don organically made designs and use the red carpet to spread the eco-fashion gospel.

As a fashion designer and PhD candidate, her research examines the relationship between consumption and red carpet production. The unfortunate dilemma with red carpet fashion is that it's made to have an impact; to be worn once and discarded once an event is over. I had a look at a number of McCorkill's designs and one dress in particular really stood out. It was fashioned from leftover silks and the full length of fabric is elegantly draped over one's body. It's beautiful - and looks like it belongs on a Grecian goddess. I loved it 'cos it would look stunning on someone with a tiny figure... or someone with junk in their trunk. And with this simple yet elegant dress, McCorkill's eco-friendly design means minimal stitching, the recycling of fabric remnants and through the draping and disassembly element, this dress could achieve numerous looks for numerous events.

So what of those of us not destined for the red carpet but wanting to play our part in eco-fashion? One sunny afternoon I headed down to Federation Square, in the heart of Melbourne's CBD, to check out an event called The Clothing Exchange. This is where the sustainable fashion community come together to swap clothes - and move towards a greener world. No money is exchanged - but you bring your old clothes that you'd like to swap and (provided they are in good condition) you're

Click Magazine Josip Kelava Client: Click Magazine

Studio Lambada showed off a new fashion statement dress. The dress was big, bold, and geometric. A matching typeface and layout of the spread was needed to express this.

Melbourne Dance Company Josip Kelava Client: Melbourne Dance Company

When I was first approached to design the poster for the new Melbourne Dance Company, I wanted to do it a little differently. It felt cliche to use a script type, as it was used like that countless times for ballet posters.
Initially the design was just going to be used as a headline but I had to remember that dance was an expression of movement, and thus, I wanted the type to wrap around the dancer as if it was dancing on it's own. And because the type has such sharp corners, and ballet is meant to be quite sensual, I purposely wanted this contrast in the juxtaposition.
I wanted the viewer to look at the poster and let it play in their mind, both with the harshness of the type and the softness of the dancer. Just like dancing can be interpretive differently to others, I wanted to do the same for the poster. Using the different characters within the type allowed me to do this, and overall, create a visual dance in itself.

The Red Thread Josip Kelava Client: The Red Thread

Using a single piece of string, and a little Photoshop work, I wanted to create the name of the band in a very dynamic way. Initially wanted to create the whole design in black & white, but the client insisted it being in red. In the end, we were both happy with the result.

METRO POLIS

Metropolis 1920   Josip Kelava   Client: Metropolis

Metropolis 1920 comes from the industrial movement of the 1920's where skyscrapers where born. Using a double line technique, I wanted to create my own Art Deco style font that represented this era. The result is a bold, bumptious typeface with a stolidly calm disposition.

And Yet — Keetra Dean Dixon & JK Keller — Client: The Walker Art Center & Smithsonian Cooper-Hewitt, National Design Museum in New York

Layered wax work. The object is created by coating positive type forms with hot wax, layer upon layer. Then the mass is sliced open and the positive letter forms are removed.

310&311

Cordial Invitations Keetra Dean Dixon & JK Keller Photographer: Keetra Dean Dixon

Postcard series fearturing aspirational messaging.

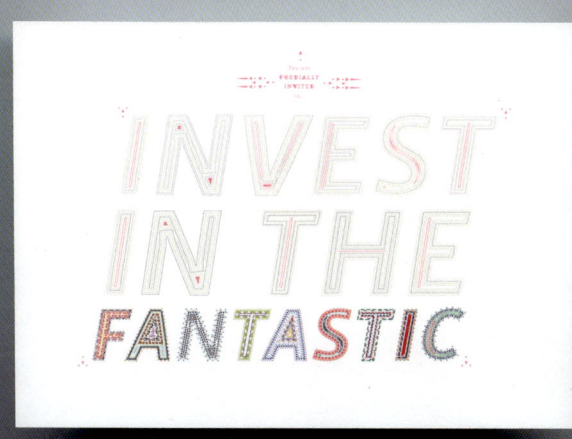
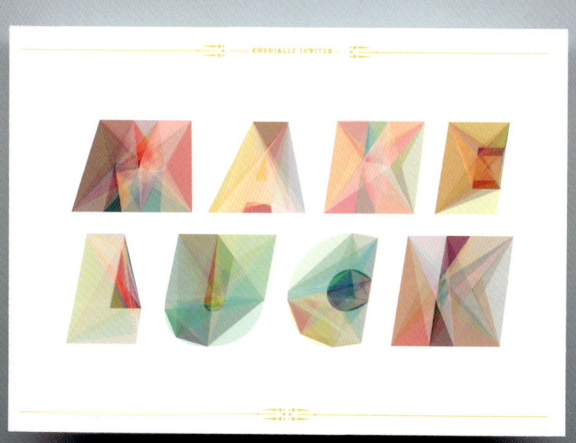

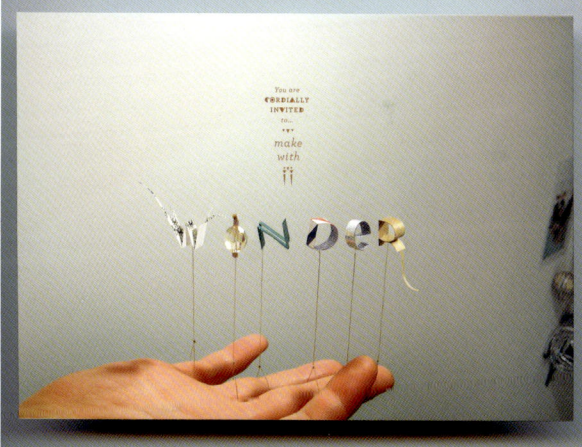
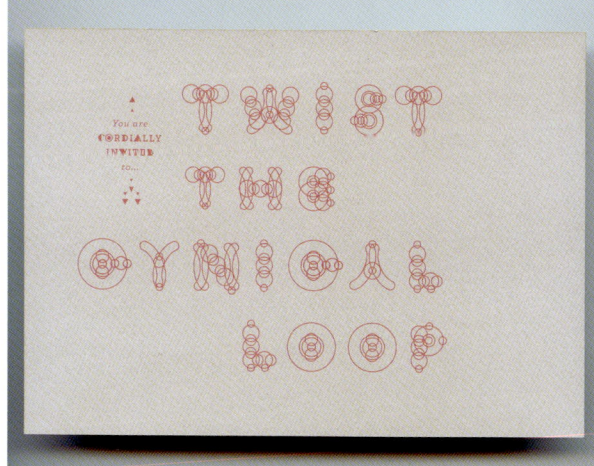

312&313

HEINEKEN BOTTLE Kissmiklos

HEINEKEN and WAMP made an exclusive tender, and invited 5 designers to design a unique bottle concept. These 2 meter high models were presented in the wamp design fair.

The Limited Night party identity concept Kissmiklos

Identity and slogan concept for a pop party series.

Artists & Fleas at Chelsea Market　　　　　　　　　　Travis W. Simon　　　　　　　　　　Client: Artists & Fleas Market
　　Others: Painting assistance by Chris Miner

The project was a rush job for a repeat customer, Artists & Fleas Market. They opened a Spring Pop-up Shop inside Chelsea Market on the West side of Manhattan. I had help with everything from a fellow sign painter Chris Miner. In just under a week we manged to design, recycle the old panels, paint and install all of them before they opened. We used 1Shot sign painters enamel to do all of the painting.

Barbara's Home Travis W. Simon

A typographic piece I made as a gift. Pen and Ink on hot press stock

Build It By Hand, Build It For Life Travis W. Simon

A glass panel I painted for an Art show. Using 1Shot sign painters enamel and a few days drying time, I wanted to create a small sample of everything I can do with sign painting in one piece.

Crest Hardware 50th Anniversary Redesign   Travis W. Simon   Client: Crest Hardware of Brooklyn, NY

Crest Hardware contacted me to redesign and paint over all the old vinyl signs they had done back in the early 90's. We recycled a lot of the old materials and modernized the aesthetics a bit using their new logo (not designed by me) and highlighting their new features. We also made some new interior isle signs and directional signs. We are currently working on adding more and helping to redesign parts of the actual store.

Lavai Maria   Travis W. Simon   Client: Crest Hardware of Brooklyn, NY

Lavai Maria is a wonderful little dress shop in Williamsburg Brooklyn. They feature custom designed and vintage altered clothing and accessories. I used the existing logo with some minor changes for the store front window and address number painting. The A-frame I painted a year ago and recently added a few more street signs to their collection with the opening of their new location.

Ragazza Script Yani Arabena & Guille Vizzari

Ragazza Script isn't just another display typeface. It honors the greatest handwriting skills but in a different way. Although It doesn't represent any traditional calligraphy style, it is still part of that expressive world.
With more than 1000 glyphs, and taking advantage of the Opentype features, Ragazza is full of personality. When in use, it gives a feel very close to ornamental Copperplate mixed with some kind of modern «high-contrast» typeface. Lots of alternates, swashes and initial capitals are the spine of this face, assuring almost infinite combination possibilities.
The early forms that would eventually lead to what Ragazza is today, began as a college project –around 2006– in the context of the «Hyperfuente» exercise developed during Typography 2, chair E. Longinotti, at the University of Buenos Aires. But that seed would never stop growing. Since then a lot of work had been made to take that initial project to a professional quality level.
Ragazza Script is perfect for headlines and short phrases.It is the brand new modern script, designed by Guille Vizzari and published by Latinotype.

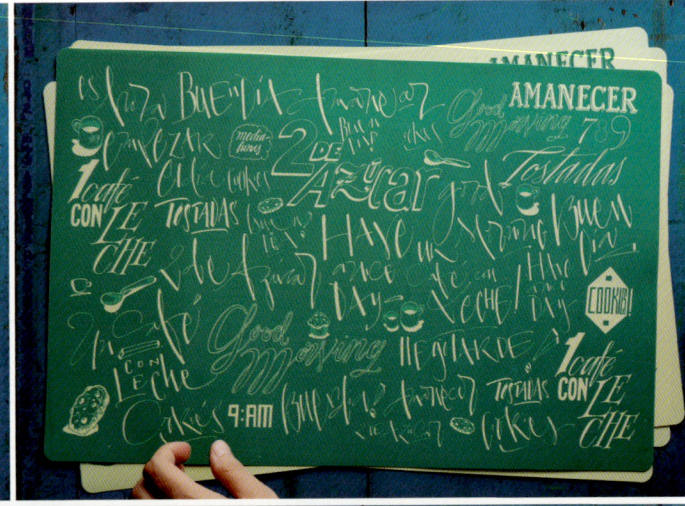
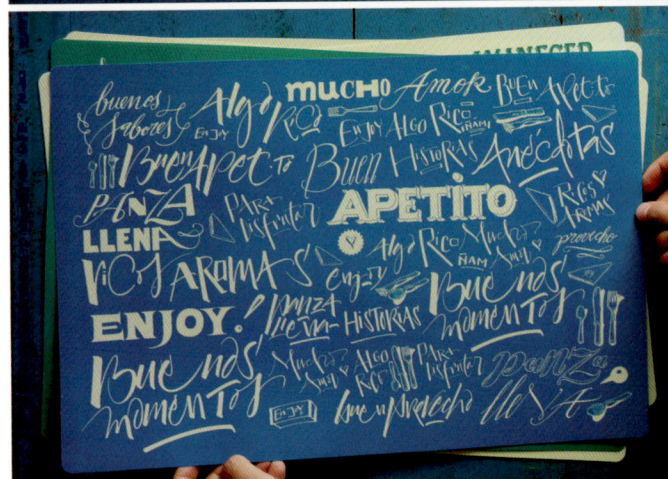

BZP Placemates Yani Arabena & Guille Vizzari Creative Director: Ezequiel Karpf
Client: BZP Bazaar

Placemate designs for BZP Bazaar, Buenos Aires, Argentina.

324&325

Tienda de Café Yani Arabena & Guille Vizzari Creative Director: María Laura Leo
Client: Tienda de Café

Calligraphy, lettering and little tiny illustrations to be aplied on coffee cups.

Cafés
Recuerdos
Experiencias

**GOOD TYPOGRAPHY IS INVISIBLE /
BAD TYPOGRAPHY IS EVERYWHERE**

PRESENTING A SERIES OF WORKSHOPS FOR SECOND YEAR GRAPHIC DESIGN PATHWAY STUDENTS LOOKING AT THE FUNDAMENTALS OF TYPOGRAPHY AND MOVABLE TYPE, INCLUDING LETTERPRESS AND TYPESETTING. WORKSHOPS BEGIN IN APRIL AND WILL TAKE PLACE AT BUCKS NEW COLLEGE, HIGH WYCOMBE. FOR MORE INFORMATION, SPEAK TO PAUL PLOWMAN OR REGISTER YOUR INTEREST BY EMAILING INFO@WORDSAREPICTURES.CO.UK

bucks new university

Good Typography is Invisible / Bad Typography is Everywhere   Craig Ward   Client: Bucks New University

A poster created to stir up interest ahead of a short workshop I conducted on moveable type at my former university.

Negative beats Positive — Craig Ward — Photographer: Bill Wadman

Part of a large campaign for the AIDS charity (RED) pushing for a end to children being born with AIDS by 2015.

Wish You Were Here Craig Ward

Created as a wall decal for London based advertising agency Elvis.

You Blow Me Away — Craig Ward — Photographer: Jason Tozer

An experimental piece of kinetic typography, initially conceived as a legibility experiment.

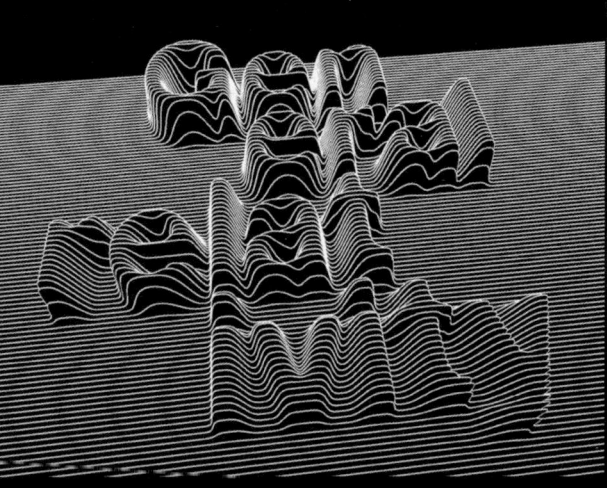
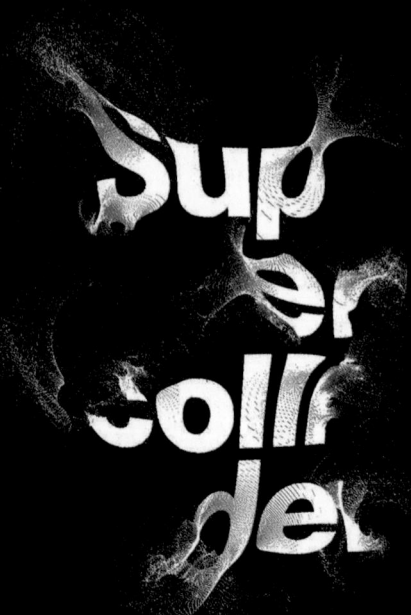

The Bulk of Reality — Craig Ward

An ongoing exploration into the ideas and terminology behind theoretical physics.